AF755422

CLINICAL PSYCHOLOGY

CLINICAL PSYCHOLOGY

K.C. Shukla
Tara Chand

Commonwealth

Clinical Psychology

© Reserved

Edition : 2017

ISBN 81-7169-908-1

Published by :
COMMONWEALTH PUBLISHERS
4831/24, Prahlad Street,
Ansari Road, Darya Ganj,
New Delhi - 110002
Ph. : 23275511, 23257835
e-mail : commonwealthbooks@gmail.com

Typesetting by :
Rishu Computers
Delhi

Printed at :
Divine Digital Press
Delhi

PREFACE

Psychology specifically directed towards clinical studies and remedies comprises this subject of this book. The material used is mostly borrowed from the foreign sources due to lack of Indian material.

Personality is one of those things which it is easier to appreciate than define. It is the whole human being considered in relation to the society in which he lives. It is somewhat different from the individuality which exists independently of the social situation.

Personality appears to depend on a number of qualities, physical, intellectual, emotional, social, moral and spiritual. It is the sum of the reactions to the master motives of the average person with whom there is inevitable comparison.

The physical qualities are shown by his health and energy, his appearance, expression and habits.

The intellectual qualities are shown by his capability in a vast number of directions.

The emotional qualities are shown by his spirit, cheerfulness, enthusiasm, industry and thrust.

Social qualities include all the things the average man likes in social life. Kindness, co-operation, adaptability, tolerance etc., etc.

Moral qualities include reliability, honesty, thoroughness.

Spiritual qualities include the material acts, idealism, love, sympathy, forgiveness, respect for God, interest in the future and welfare of mankind.

A consideration of what has already been said indicates that it is the resultant of the total forces concerned with the formation of the mind, the heredity together with the personal experience of the individual as shown by his relations towards his fellows and their institutions.

It is hoped the book will be found very useful by the people of the medical profession besides by researchers and professors of psychology.

K.C. Shukla
Tara Chand

CONTENTS

	Preface	v
Chapter		Pages
1.	Processes of the Nervous System	1
2.	Motives and the Instincts	14
3.	The Security Instinct	20
4.	The Sex Instinct	33
5.	The Urge for Power	39
6.	The Instinct of Herd	46
7.	Frustration and Conflict	55
8.	The Desire for Submission	60
9.	Continuance of Conflict	73
10.	Personality	84
11.	Dreams and Human Behaviour	90
12.	Illusion in the Psychotherapeutic Enterprise	95
13.	Applications of Buddhism in Mental Health Care	113
14.	Buddhism and Behaviour Change : Implications for Therapy	134
15.	Bankei – Seventeenth Century Japanese Social Worker?	147
16.	Meditation : Psychology and Human Experience	154
17.	The New Religions and Psychotherapy : Similarities and Differences	176
18.	Psychotherapy and Techniques of Transformation	194
19.	Therapy and Beyond : Concluding Thoughts	210

1

PROCESSES OF THE NERVOUS SYSTEM

Some psychologists hold that in considering mental processes the nervous system may be ignored altogether and it is certainly true that many succeed in the practice of psychotherapy with a surprisingly small elementary knowledge of its basal workings. Like so many other subjects, psychology may be studied without detailed reference to the fundamental processes on which it depends. A man may even make a wireless set without knowing the fundamental process involved in the action of a wireless valve. Many good practical electricians knew remarkably little about the fundamentals of their craft. In a modern world it is scarcely possible to be complete master of the theory and practice of a craft, but it is all the more desirable that the theorists and practitioners should get together, otherwise both may go wrong. It used to be considered that the brain might be looked upon as the organ of the mind, but later knowledge in the field of therapeutics has shown that the structural, disease or malfunction of the brain may result in many mental derangements which earlier were considered beyond the reach of physical processes.

One of the earliest recognised of these states was general paralysis of the insane in which typically the subjects suffer from remarkable delusions especially those of grandeur and exaltation. Frequently they identify themselves with notable persons. This condition is now known to be produced by the effects of the spirochæte of syphilis on the brain. We now know that tumours of the frontal lobe may produce mental states indistinguishable from other forms of insanity and that removal of such tumours may relieve the disturbed mental state. Striking too is the effect of thyroid extract on the mentality of a cretin child whose thyroid has failed to grow normally. The child which might have been an idiotic dwarf may, through the administration of thyroid extract, become a normal member of society.

More recently cases of schizophrenia or split-personality which hitherto have been considered in the realm of immaterial psychology, have been shown to be cured by causing nervous shock by means of large doses of insulin or electricity applied to the head.

Thus, we see that it is really less possible than formerly to justify the separation of Psychology from the study of the nervous system, indeed, the more we become acquainted with the activity of the latter the more it becomes evident that the processes of the mind show themselves not to be essentially different from the processes of the nervous system whose chief function is to protect the animal against pain and adapt it to its environment. It must, however, be understood that this admission is not to be taken as an acceptance of Behaviourism.

The Reflex

This section is given in summary as most readers of this volume will have already read more detailed description in text-books of Physiology.

The nervous system is built up of neurones, that is, nervecells with their processes which carry messages to and from it. The cells are stationed in the brain, spinal cord and the ganglia of the nervous system, but their processes collected together in bundles form the nerves which are seen as white cords throughout the body. The neurones are the structural units.

The physiological or functional unit of the nervous system of all animals is the reflex. A simple example of this type of reaction is seen in the *protective spinal reflex*. If the foot is pricked, it is withdrawn. A nerve impulse is set up in the skin by the prick, is transmitted by afferent nerves to the spinal cord whence another impulse is transmitted to the muscles controlling the leg and foot. That the response is not in any way dependent on the brain is seen by the fact that it takes place in the body of animals whose brain has been removed but whose spinal cord is retained, while its independence of consciousness is seen by its occurrence in a sleeping person.

If the stimulus is sufficiently strong there is spread to other efferent pathways and not only may the leg of the opposite side be removed, but the forelimbs also. It is found also that although one stimulus may be insufficient to provoke stimulus a repetition of the stimuli may be effective. These facts are commonly explained as being that the strength of the stimulus overcomes synaptic resistance, i.e., the junction between neurones, in the same sort of way that a strong electric current will jump a spark gap, but it may be dependent on the accumulation of chemical substances at the synapses.

A still higher type of reflex is that concerned with posture. By means of *postural reflexes* an animal maintains its normal standing position, its head in relation to the earth and its body in relation to its head.

The impulses concerned in standing arise from the effect of gravity tending to bend the limbs and to stretch certain tendons. This stretching sets up impulses which pass up to the spinal cord to Deiters' nucleus in the upper part of the medulla and impulses are sent back to the muscles to cause them to contract.

The impulses concerned with the position of the head arise from the weight of minute particles of chalk hanging from hair-like processes of certain cells in the otolithic cavities of the internal ear, those relating the body to the head arise in the muscles of the neck. All impulses concerned are co-related in the mid-brain whence they are relayed to the appropriate muscles. These reactions take place in animals deprived of consciousness and conscious activity by removal of its cerebral hemispheres. Such animals not only can maintain the standing posture automatically but will walk, run or gallop if stood on a platform which can be moved at appropriate speeds.

Conditioned Reflexes

A still higher type of reflex involves consciousness and the cerebrum. This is the *conditioned reflex* described by Pavlov who took.advantage of the fact that a hungry dog secretes saliva when it is shown food. In the classical experiment a bell was rung each time a dog was fed and eventually it was found that the dog secreted saliva when the bell was rung although the food was not presented. Such reactions are commonly seen in pet dogs when the dinner gong in sounded.

The evidence that the response, although it involved consciousness in its formation, is not eventually one of conscious activity, is that drawn from the experiment of repeatedly ringing the bell half an hour before the food is presented. The dog then secretes saliva half an hour after the ringing of the bell. If, however, during the interval the dog is disturbed by an extraneous stimulus, saliva is at once secreted showing that there has been some sort of restraining influence or inhibition (known as internal inhibition) of the response which is released by the extraneous stimulus. The emptying of the bladder during excitement in a puppy during house training is probably a similar release of an inhibited reflex, the inhibition not yet being very strong.

A dog can be taught also that certain stimuli are associated with no food and it responds accordingly.

In all reflexes repetition makes the response more immediate as a result of the reduction of the resistance of the synapses between the neurones. Repetition also tends to fix conditioned reflexes.

In the formation of the conditioned reflexes there is also an association in time, a fact which suggests that when two self-propagating nerve impulses enter the nervous system, at once or at a short interval of time, they tend to meet. We have already noted that when we associate two ideas or happenings it is usually because of a similar coincidence or sequence in time.

It will at once be realised that many of our actions depend on similar reflexes and also many of the actions to which lower animals have been trained. Where we put our railway ticket, the way we hold our pen or knife and fork have all been thought out but eventually, as a result of repetition, the action becomes automatic or reflex. From time to time we have to excuse ourselves for certain actions which have been done "absentmindedly" from force of habit. For some ten years the author lectured from twelve to one o'clock and thereafter had lunch, but circumstances led to a change of the lecture hour to eleven o'clock. On two occasions in the ensuing three months he found himself an hour too early in the lunch-room at the other end of the building before realising the mistake.

Voluntary Movement and Reaction Times

It is possible to study certain reflexes with great accuracy, not by observing the muscle response but by recording the electrical changes in the nerve, the time of stimulation and the time of the arrival of the impulse to the muscle. By similar means it is possible to measure that exact speed at which nerve impulses travel along nerves. This varies in different nerves and is from 6 to 120 metres per second. It is found, however, that the time taken in reflexes is appreciably longer and this is accounted for by assuming that there is a delay or resistance at the synapse or junction between the neurones concerned. It is, moreover, found that if the reflex is repeated several times, the time of response shortens presumably because the delay at the synapse becomes less. This is known as *facilitation* and obviously is of great importance in those reflexes which we acquire and which become very rapid from habitual use.

It is possible to study voluntary responses in a similar way. The time of stimulation and the time of response is recorded and it is found that the time taken to respond is increased the longer the nerves along which the impulses have to pass and the greater the number of neurones involved. It is found too that voluntary responses obey the same laws which have been found to apply to reflexes, not only so, but drugs such as bromides and strychnine which respectively diminish and increase, reflex responses have a similar effect on voluntary reaction times.

This similarity between reflexes and voluntary responses suggests that the fundamental processes may be more alike than is generally recognised. We are familiar too with the fact that great skill may be acquired by habitual movements. These observations are of interest in any consideration of the exact nature of voluntary movement. It is usual to consider such movement as commencing activity of the Betz cells of the motor area of the cerebrum but what stimulus stimulates them is nebulous. It may be that the majority if not all voluntary movements depend for their stimulus on the external environment. This would account for our making any movement at any given time.

The exact response, however, to the stimulus is profoundly influenced by the introduction of conscious reasoning between the arrival of the stimulus and the execution of the movement.

Speech

There is one movement which is of special interest – namely, vocal speech. Speech is a movement which involves the action of the muscles of respiration, of the larynx and of the mouth. It may, under certain circumstances, be replaced by movements of other parts of the body, such as a nod of the head. We call it a voluntary act.

At the same time it is also agreed that speech may not infrequently be quite involuntary. Certain individuals may respond to certain stimuli by swearing. It is common parlance that a man may speak without thinking. We even find Shakespeare causing Polonius to give advice to his son :

> Give thy thoughts no tongue,
> Nor any unproportioned thought his act.

In the pathological state of aphasia, it is not infrequently found that the individual may be quite unable to answer a question, yet he may still swear when stimulated or repeat poetry which, as we say, he has "learnt by heart" in his early years. Or he may be able to say such words as he might say automatically. There is then evidence that certain speech at least may be quite automatic – and that such speech may be produced in a way which is strictly analogous to the formation of a conditioned reflex.

By repetition speech becomes fixed. It has already been remarked that repetition is of enormous importance in relation to nervous activity, and we are familiar with the importance of repetition in teaching and learning. Many of us recall passages of verse or prose which we learnt at school and still recall the amount of repetition which was necessary to fix it in our memories, but now it seems to be fixed indelibly. We just need one or two key words to make us remember a whole passage.

If rapid speech is analysed as a movement it is often possible to discover the original stimulus. This is the essence of the value of rapid examination in the witness-box. The witness, we say, gives himself away. What does he give away? He gives an insight, as we say, into his mind, he indicates the habitual paths of previous stimuli. It is as if we were riding a horse and the horse wished to go in a certain direction. By its behaviour we can usually analyse the animal's mind and give good reason for its preference for one way rather than another.

But suppose that we ourselves are about to make a hasty reply. The speech is on the tip of the tongue when we receive another stimulus, we see someone perhaps. Where is the speech? It remains in our thoughts. We imagine the result of our saying it and compare it with past memories as if we had heard the speech. We have formed a cycle of thought.

Such cycles of thought are exactly like any other habit, in that they appear to establish definite pathways. It is indeed generally agreed that there is such a thing as a habit of thought. Systems of memory training, such as Pelmanism, have for their basis the establishment of groups of words or ideas, so that the mention of one word will automatically call up others of the group. We often say that whenever we think of one thing we think of something else, or we say when we are telling stories – "that reminds me of one". Thus, it is seen that habits of speech and habits of thought are closely interrelated and are probably playing a larger part in human affairs than is generally realised.

Education as a Reflex Building Process

However much some may dislike the idea, it will be generally admitted that one of the fruits of education is habit forming. The constant curbing of natural desires leads to the establishment of certain lines of conduct upon which society looks with favour. However much we may covet the food of a neighbour, we do not steal it, or however much he annoys us we do not necessarily fight him. Children are sent to a certain school because of the pattern of boy which it tends to produce. Study along certain lines tends to develop certain types of mind, while those who specialise in child guidance tell us how the child's whole conduct may be influenced by teaching him to play in certain ways. It is not the purpose of this book to discuss the advantages and disadvantages of universal state education but it is certainly evident that it would tend to level mankind, but in doing so would tend to curb the adventurous spirits who seek to strike out in new paths.

It is a strange trait in human nature that at quite an early age there is a great tendency to establish self-education along certain lines. The newspapers read, the wireless items listened to, show evidence of the desire along certain political, sociological or cultural avenues and disinterestedness in the views of others who may hold the opposite opinion. Democracy with its freedom of thought and speech is characterised by its allowing a very large amount of freedom provided it does not interfere with the general peace. In more purely educational spheres it would seem that the hereditary aspect, or early parental influences, plays a considerable part in determining learnings in certain directions, although it is well recognised that the immature mind may be greatly influenced by certain teachers. The truth of this statement has been amply borne out by the remarkable influence of mass education in totalitarian states.

Conditioned Sensation

The phenomenon of conditioning is usually held to apply only to movement or activity but it is easy to demonstrate that sensation may also be conditioned. In medicine this is very important in relation to pain and the physiological reaction and reflexes thereto. Pain is a sensation which normally results from a certain quality of stimulation, usually that which produces, or is liable to produce, definite tissue damage.

Thus, not only does stimulation of the eyeball lead to the eyelids closing, but also any sudden movement or sound. A blow apparently aimed at the head will bring about closure of the eyes and in man an attempt to ward it off. But the reactions caused in such ways are not confined to responses of which we are conscious. A pinprick anywhere on the body leads to constriction of the vessels of the skin, but so also does a threat of a prick provided the subject is convinced that the pricking may be carried out.

The occurrence of such a response was first demonstrated by Mosso with his plethysmograph, an apparatus by which the volume of the hand may be measured. He showed that many forms of mental activity, especially those associated with fear, may cause a constriction of the blood-vessels of the hand. Is necessary to emphasise that a large number of afferent stimuli may be conditioned and produce the same response as pain.

A common and closely related phenomenon is the pain which becomes associated with injury and which is so important in surgery. After injury, pain associated with movement is very common and persistent, but it is now well recognised that the pain may persist much longer than its initial cause. This pain is seen in pet animals. A dog if injured may continue limping indefinitely, especially if it has received specially agreeable treatment during its injury. Occasionally when chasing a cat or a mouse it "forgets" its injury and the limp disappears.

Pain on movement may occur in injury to the foot, knee, or in sciatica, but once established such pain may be extremely difficult to cure, especially if the subject benefits in any way from having the pain. The pain is commonly an excuse for absence from work. It is now well recognised that after injury, recovery is much more likely to occur if a lump sum is paid by an insurance company, than if a lesser sum is paid at intervals.

There are many varieties of this conditioned pain, a doctor may not have the typical symptoms of gall-stones until they have been definitely diagnosed by X-ray, or he may develop all the symptoms of cancer until he is convinced, by continued life, that the symptoms from which he suffers have a simpler cause. A man who thinks he has exposed himself to venereal disease may develop an abnormal sensation in, or even inflammation of, his penis.

Fear is a phenomenon closely related to conditioned sensation, but is entirely a threat and may or may not have been associated with the sensation of pain. The emotion of fear is experienced in relation to any kind of threat to security and is therefore dealt with in a subsequent section.

Conditioned Fatigue

This condition can scarcely be appreciated by those who have not experienced it, but it is a perfectly normal phenomenon. It is, however, an important factor in convalescence and unemployment.

A patient who has been ill, suffers extremely from a sense of exhaustion and fatigue which is very considerable. This is experienced typically after influenza, and still more so after a major abdominal operation in which case it may continue for months. It occurs in all classes of workers after prolonged unemployment. Unless the subject is expecting and understands it, it is most distressing and depressing. Not only so, it is extremely difficult to continue to make oneself "do things", but serious illness may be suspected, or the patient may fall a victim to the many subtle advertisements which claims to restore vitality.

It is not to be wondered, therefore, that in many this sense of fatigue becomes associated with a quite small amount of work. Many patients tell their doctors that they simply cannot do this or that, say walk five miles, yet to do so is within the reach of every person who is not suffering from any diagnosable ailment other than fatigue. That tired feeling and fatigue complex are very closely related to work shyness and psychologically to a fear of the sense of fatigue and an escape from the reality of work.

It seems probable that conditioned fatigue is a factor in premature senility. There comes a time usually about the age of forty when a man can no longer be a first-class athlete. Few men find they have the time and energy to indulge in the more active sports after this age and many get out of practice. They hate to be beaten by younger men and some get so depressed that they give up games altogether with the result that they get worse and become old before their time. At this stage many become patients but only require being properly told that they are quite healthy but out of condition.

It seems also most likely that the disinclination of many to do mental work is due to a similar train of circumstances.

The treatment of conditioned pain or fatigue is difficult, for the doctor may by the slightest indication that the symptom complained of is "not real" simply cause the patient to go to another doctor who is more sympathetic and often less scrupulous. Commonly too the patients come to hate the doctor who genuinely may be trying to cure them by encouraging them to try to neglect the pain. The hate may spread to a hatred of all doctors and a cure can then only be possible by a non-medical man who admits the pain but claims to cure it by treatment which can only have a psychological value. Electricity, mysterious appliances, manipulations, faith-healing have their adherents and if used with sufficient ceremony, effect cures. The most satisfactory procedure is generally for the family doctor to pass on the patient to a consultant whose name, fee and address contribute to the success of the treatment.

It is essential in treatment to obtain the confidence and co-operation of the patient for it must be remembered (and this psychotherapy has taught the older physicians) that the ailment is real, and that it is as much the doctor's business to treat it as it is to treat an existing pathological lesion. The blunt suggestion that the patient is malingering, or treating the patient as if she is, by some variety of solitude treatment may produce such resentment that the cure may become even more difficult. Exhortation, combined if possible with incentive to recovery, such as pointing out that the complaint is usual, combined with a modicum of sympathy and attention are needed. Sometimes all the wiles of the quack are needed to assist and the honest doctor must not forget that the patient goes to him to be cured, and if he does so he is not dishonest simply because he does not confide the true nature of the complaint to his patient or his friends.

Rôle of Heredity in Reflex Processes

Fortunately we know that all persons educated alike, in as far as this is possible, have not the same reactions, for we are products not only of our environment and education but also of our heredity.

It is commonly remarked that children have a physical likeness to their parents and this may give rise to a functional likeness, for example, in gait which we know is largely reflex. It is easy to imagine, too, that just as the configuration of the head may approximate to that of the parent so may that of the brain and that similarly, detailed cerebral structure may also bear some resemblance. While it is common knowledge that a child may "take after" one or other of his parents it should, however, be pointed out that the functional resemblance may be basal rather than superficial and that many of the qualities of mind required for worldly success are, as pointed out by Keith, also those of a really successful housewife. Similarly, basal deficiencies such as lack of perseverance may lead to failure in otherwise capable persons in any walk of life.

In many cases the individuals of outstanding attainment have become so as the result of their heredity, for as we say, the quality has been "bred in the bone" whether it be art, music or fighting. It is also common experience that great clowns, acrobats, mathematicians, musicians, soldiers, are descended from ancestry with similar specialised capabilities. Unfortunately, we usually only hear of the most distinguished in a particular line. We may be familiar with two musicians Bach, who were father and son, but there were many other musical members of the family; indeed, there was an all Bach instrumental band. But correspondingly some have the greatest difficulty in learning some subjects. Thus, mathematics to some are easy, but to others difficult. We may imagine that every individual is more readily educated along certain lines than along others, indeed, vocational testing indicates that this generalisation is probably true.

2

MOTIVES AND THE INSTINCTS

Closely allied to the reflexes are the instincts, which may be described as the innate tendencies of animals to behave in a certain way and are common to all animals, amongst which they may, however, differ in detail. Lloyd Morgan has suggested that a criterion of instinctive behaviour is serviceability on the first occasion for the welfare of the individual and his species, and he has emphasised its dependence on parts of the nervous system lower than the cerebrum and that intelligence, which depends on the cerebrum, supplies the finishing touches, the net result being a joint product of both yet each remains genetically distinguishable.

On the instincts depends the life of the animal world, and on them the preservation of the individual and the preservation of the race to which he belongs. The universal instincts therefore are those concerned with food and drink, protection and reproduction upon which all life depends.

These instincts bear a very striking resemblance to reflexes and are as truly fixed in the nervous system of animals as reflexes. They differ indeed, only in the speed of the reaction and that the response is an action and not merely a movement or secretion but a complicated action. In the case of thirst, we know exactly the mechanisms which are concerned in producing the intense desire for fluid. The sensation results from a drying of the specialised nerve-endings of the tongue which is the result of the withdrawing of water from them. This withdrawal may result from the local application of substances such as salt or alcohol or from increased concentration of the blood itself which is the result of loss of water from the skin. In regard to hunger we know less of the exact mechanism concerned, but we believe that it is associated with increased tension on certain nerve-endings in the stomach wall. Hunger and thirst are well known to be two of the most compelling sensations known. Fear of hunger is, by association, equally compelling but in a civilised world more rare.

It must at the same time be admitted that it is difficult to imagine that the instinct which causes an animal to hoard food is dependent on any afferent impulses. Animal psychologists, however, tell us that such hoarded food is commonly forgotten by non-hibernating animals such as dogs.

Of the exact origin of the reproductive instinct we know little but that sexual desire is exaggerated in such states as adrenal disease, prostate enlargement, increased external temperature, a full urinary bladder, or mechanical stimulation of the penis, clitoris of nipples, while it is reduced in fatigue, hypothyroidism and in cold. All these states indicate that instinctive desire has a physical basis, but admittedly many factors, many of which are psychological, go to the making of the sexual urge which is undoubtedly a most powerful motive in human behaviour.

It is convenient to consider those instincts which are concerned with nutrition, self-preservation and reproduction as the primary instincts since without them the species must necessarily perish. They are indeed essential to life itself. In a modern world, nutrition and self-preservation may be considered as the security instinct.

In addition there are others which may be termed secondary since they are not possessed by all but which are so powerful and such important motives in civilised life that they require special consideration. They are the herd instinct which tends to make individuals act and think in groups or communities, the power instinct which urges some individuals to gain superiority over their fellows and the spiritual instinct by which man is urged on towards an idealist and immaterial goal. Analysed to their ultimate, these secondary instincts are not, however, entirely separable from the primary, for example, the herd and power instincts contribute materially to the supply of food and to protection.

The primary and secondary instincts certainly supply the master motives of life for the average human being and their satisfaction gives mental happiness and physical content. If their natural outlet is frustrated, there may be tension, discomfort or actual pain, but the extent to which these occur depends largely on the physical make-up of the individual concerned and his environmental conditions. Different individuals vary very much in the extent to which they are consciously and unconsciously affected by their instincts and the relative effects of the different instincts also vary. In some, certain instincts appear to absorb almost all the energy of the individual. Sometimes the power or the spiritual urge take first place and leave a sexless shadow with scarcely the physical power or mental courage to defend himself or his ideals. This may be true of nations as well as of individuals.

The exact mechanism by which the instincts demand satisfaction has long been a centre point of dispute. Freudians look upon the instincts as being possessed of a kind of energy which like that of a pent-up fire or an ever flowing spring tends to make it surmount or get round all objects (especially the conscious self) in its way. The average biologist sees no difficulty in looking upon the instinctive mechanism as being driven by certain sensory stimuli in the same way as many reflexes which are in constant operation in the body. The absence of exact knowledge regarding the exact origin of the force need not, however, hamper our acceptance of the force any more than the acceptance of electricity although we do not know its nature.

When life begins, the child is conscious only of comfort and pleasure derived largely from feeding and excretion, but gradually it becomes aware of a world of reality other than itself which may bring to it discomfort and pain. There can be little doubt that the lives of the less civilised members of the community, whether rich or poor, are guided largely by their simple desire regarding food and comfort and their energies are devoted almost entirely to their attainment.

Gradually, however, many other instincts develop with their attendant emotions. McDougall has classified the instincts and their attendant emotions as follows :

1. Escape from danger	Fear.
2. Combat	Anger.
3. Repugnance	Disgust.
4. Parental protection of young	Parental feeling.
5. Curiosity	Adventure.
6. Self-assertive	Superiority.
7. Self-abasement	Subjection.
8. Cry of distress	Helplessness.
9. Sex	Sexual desire.
10. Herd	Loneliness.
11. Food seeking	Appetite.
12. Hoarding	Feeling of ownership.
13. Construction	Feeling of creativeness.
14. Laughter	Amusement.

In view of the fact that McDougall did so much to emphasise the importance of the instincts as determining factors in conduct, it is interesting to remark that he considered the first seven as yielding the most definite primary emotions and as secondary several, notably sex, which modern psychotherapists consider more important. It will be noted too, that he does not include reference to any spiritual instinct or the emotion of anxiety. This observation goes to emphasise the essential difference between the outlooks of the academic and medical psychologists. McDougall's distinct contribution was the relating of the emotions to the instincts.

It must be obvious that all such classifications are purely arbitrary and in their conception are of necessity coloured by the experience of their author. Some have gone further and included the innate tendencies as instincts.

These instincts as set forth by McDougall are not, however, of equal importance in human affairs and while recognising their existence, for present medical consideration in this volume the primary and secondary instincts are all that need be considered.

The essential problem which concerns medicine is the satisfaction of the instincts once they have developed and in this both the individual and society are involved. Moreover, there may be considerable difficulty in reconciling the demands of each. It has now been quite clearly proved that an untold amount of physical and mental illness has resulted from lack of frank acceptance and explanation of the facts. In this, psychotherapy has proved itself an invaluable branch of medicine although at the same time it has, as was almost inevitable, tended to stress unduly the sexual aspect because in time of peace the other essential instincts, the security instincts, are usually satisfied. The good doctor whose therapeutics are not limited to the confines of clinical science has always practised psychotherapy.

It has not been adequately stressed that this frankness has not at the same time extended to society. Modern civilisation makes such demands on the physical reserves of the individual, especially on those in places of importance, that they who ought to guide have their primary instincts so attenuated by fatigue or senility, or are possessed of such undue preponderance of the secondary instincts that they completely fail to recognise the strength and power of the primary instincts except in their gross manifestations and thus inflict many gross injustices on their fellows in whom the primary instincts are more strongly developed. In some quarters there is a tendency to ascribe this attenuation to superior conscious moral influences in conflict with "the sins of the flesh". This is, of course, in a few instances true, but more commonly it is due to the paralysing influence of the asexual old women of both sexes whose enfeebled spirits seek, in the name of religion, to rob the robust and youthful of all the healthy appetites they have long since lost. The official church which depends on their patronage cannot afford to ignore them and therefore has lost much of its influence upon the lives of the people at a time when good practical religion, which has persisted throughout the ages with and without the church, flourishes in our midst as never before.

In medicine the influence of the instincts and urges is overwhelming. We see acute illness produced by continued anxiety or fear lest they are not satisfied and, if their unsatisfaction appears certain – although it may not necessarily be so – acute depression and melancholy may occur. In the more robust there may be resentment, anger and even mania. So acute may these reactions become that the individual may require institutional treatment, and the fact that melancholia and mania may alternate from time to time in the same patient indicates the similarity of their origin. The states may occur in relation to practically all the instincts or urges and must be looked upon simply as excessive reactions to what are normal emotions in persons who chance to have inherited mentalities (nervous systems) which are inadequate to adapt them to the variabilities of a modern world.

It is now becoming abundantly evident that the instincts may be profoundly affected by chemical substances – notably extracts of the ductless glands. In animals it has been shown possible to reverse the natural sexual instincts from female to male, and in women suffering from virilism, in which the mental outlook like some of the secondary sexual characteristics, becomes male, it has been found possible to refeminise the woman by removing part of the adrenal glands. The whole idea of instinctive behaviour being dependent on chemical substances is indeed revolutionary, and where it may lead to gives ample scope for imaginative thought.

3

THE SECURITY INSTINCT

The term "security instinct" is convenient as it includes the various instincts which are essential for the preservation of the individual and are possessed by all animals. They include the instincts which make animals nourish and protect themselves against who may harm them or their food supply.

The security instincts are commonly overlooked in books on psychology except that in war-time they may conflict with the demands of the herd or community which insists that a man may ignore his personal security in the greater interests of the community. As pointed out, especially by Horner, there is little doubt that in times of peace, the security instincts play an important part in determining the vocation of the individual, and doubt regarding their satisfaction is a common cause of anxiety and social unrest. Security has always been an almost determining factor of the foreign policy of nations as recent history has amply shown. Most nations do not think of war as a possible reality until their security is actually threatened, rather they prefer to avoid the disagreeable thought and prefer to live in a phantasy of peaceful neutrality!

In a modern world security is usually synonymous with financial provision for bad times, illness or old age. Until comparatively recently this was denied to those whose incomes were small, but a considerable remedy has been achieved through the advent of sickness, old age and unemployment benefits.

There can be little doubt that security is an important factor in selecting a vocation, especially one in which promotion occurs through the length of service and some sort of pension. The number of such protected posts are steadily growing as various corporations and public utility companies increase their staffs. Too often it is forgotten that such provision tends to sap the vitality and initiative of the employee who tends to sit back and wait for dead men's shoes. Thrift tends to be discouraged and waste encouraged.

There is ample evidence that those who have the courage to throw security and comfort to the winds often come off best in the long-run, although admitted many who gamble in this way may find that their ability has not been equal to their courage. In no sphere of life is the balance between security and adventure so well seen as in the professions. Youth relies on its health and takes risks which are not so attractive to those of more experience. In professional life undergraduate and young graduate has to choose between years of hard work and poorly paid or non-paid work with little leisure and taking better paid commercial posts with fewer prospects but which give him free evenings and more time for social contacts. At this stage his friends in business have many obvious advantages and this becomes more and more evident if marriage is contemplated.

Most people in all walks of life try to mix security and adventure. Family stock-brokers recommend such procedure in relation to their clients, and even intelligent research workers commonly find that they mix researches of two types with the same general purpose. Thus, amongst the safe researches are those "on the effect of this on that" which gives a negative or positive result which may be published. This occupies over eighty per cent of our scientific journals and provides occupation for hundreds of grantees of different kinds, at least a dull occupation for their dull minds. Those, however, who gamble by trying out fresh ideas lead more interesting lives but may toil in vain.

The young man is anxious about his future, his being able to maintain a family and so on. Often the anxiety is even greater on the part of a woman on whom the care of the family chiefly falls. For this reason women prefer their husbands to be in secure posts. These anxieties tend to become exaggerated at middle age when probabilities can be calculated.

In war-time different kinds of break-downs occur through anxiety, some for the reasons given above and some from anxiety for the physical welfare of the individual and his family. In peace-time this has commonly been assured in civilised countries and the idea of inescapable danger comes somewhat as a shock. The doctor, probably more than any other outside the fighting services, is familiar with the reaction to this situation, for from time to time it falls to him to announce the necessity for a surgical operation or declare how serious the complaint is. Most practitioners admit that they have amongst their regular patients quite a number who merely need to be told that their complaint is not serious and that they have nothing to worry about. Putting the patient's mind at rest is indeed "half the battle" in therapeutics.

Amongst nations we see also the past influence of the security instincts. The typically "canniness" of the Scot is no doubt a relic of many generations when security was in jeopardy. The Germanic invasions of France were admittedly responsible for great anxiety regarding security and the national relief when the country was considered impregnable, led as an almost natural sequence to the "maginot mind" which turned out to be a fool's paradise. We are often incorrectly reminded in this connection of the ostrich who hides its head in the sand to escape danger. This is not to prevent it from being seen as most people imagine but to make itself look like a typical desert bush.

Fear

The special importance of the security instincts in medical psychology is that they give rise to fear and anxiety.

It must be understood that fear is a perfectly normal protective reaction to anything which is believed to be harmful or which is not completely understood. A puppy or a child is afraid of entering an unaccustomed room and may treat quite harmless objects with distrust. A lion may be afraid of an umbrella, horses used to be afraid of motor-cars. Intense fear of the sound made by air-raid sirens and of bombs was at first very noticeable, but familiarity and the learning of the fact that, like thunder, they are not so dangerous as they sound, often lead to an almost dangerous contempt of their significance except by those who have actually had terrifying experiences. There can be no doubt that always running to shelter tends to reduce the morale and exaggerates the fear, while having of necessity to be exposed is beneficial, however much this may be against the public interest.

Different nations have different traditional fears, fear of witch-doctors, of demons or the "evil eye". Fear of the Devil has been common until recent times. Certain puritans appear to have a fear of secular enjoyment, and so on. Some nations such as Red Indians and Japanese adopt a war paint and grotesque dress to make themselves more fearful.

Fear of the unknown shows itself in adults who are about to experience things of which they have little knowledge except that there is an element of danger. This is seen typically in regard to surgical operations or air raids. Sometimes the effect of the mental apprehension when the danger is distant is much greater than the fear when the danger is imminent. Fear of things which are known to be dangerous is common may be considered legitimate and leads to great care being taken but in some persons these fears are exaggerated as in fear of thunder and lightning, fear of deep water, fear of heights and even of motoring.

To the child the world is so much unknown and must be influenced by what he reads or is told. His giants and demons are therefore real to him until he has found out otherwise.

Since all animals have probably experienced discomfort, if not actual pain, at some time or another, by a process of conditioning many objects and circumstances become identified with pain or discomfort and many, like a threatened injury, bring about the state of fear which, in certain circumstances, can be most terrifying and compelling. Often indeed, the fear may be much more upsetting than the reality. Such fears are commonly seen in pet animals. A dog which has been accidentally injured by a pellet may cease to follow the gun or be obviously afraid of bangs. A puppy once carried in a basket for a long distance in a train or motor-car may refuse thereafter to enter a motor-car, although it may subsequently be brought to like motoring as judged by its eagerness to enter the car. It is important to remark that in the re-educating process the use of force may be necessary.

The neurotic adult never really loses many of the fears which are normal to or which he may have acquired as a child, not only so but in both man and animals the fears become extended by a process of association. The fear engendered by an air-raid siren is obviously not of the noise itself but of what it portends, and it has been observed that a dog afraid of a gun and of bangs may show signs of distaste of a siren.

Specific Phobias or Fixed Fears – A very large variety of phobias exist to which classical names have been attached. Thus, we have fears of water, of disease, especially of cancer or venereal disease, of knives, of closed spaces, of wide open spaces, of the dark, of different animals, of dirt and germs, of being alone, of leaving home, etc., etc. These phobias, or "fixations" as they are sometimes called, have commonly their origin in experience during childhood, during which the child was shut in a dark place, frightened when being bathed, when in an open space, etc., etc. The actual occurrence which originally caused the fear may, however, have been completely forgotten, but sufficient cases have now been completely analysed that there can be no doubt regarding the existence of the early fright. Some psychologists who have not succeeded in tracking down such origins to phobias believe that they have an even deeper meaning and are to be understood in terms of symbolism and interpretation (Howe). Thus, the fear of heights is claimed to occur especially in those who are ambitious but timid, claustrophobia an indication that the individual really wishes to isolate himself from the world.

Of special interest are the disease phobias which as we have said are commonly those of cancer and venereal disease. They become of special importance because unlike the other phobias they cannot be avoided. The phobia is always present and may become increasingly intense, so much so that their possessors may become acutely melancholic. This state may be aggravated by an intense sense of inferiority. Doctors themselves may be so effected, and two recent cases which have come to my notice became unfit for work for prolonged periods. There is evidence that many of the fears have their origin in guilt which is discussed in a later section.

The fear of mice has been given a sexual significance and, it is suggested, is common in women because the animal lives in a hole. Such psychologists ignore the possibility that the animal might seek refuge up the skirts as they say it seldom happens. The woman does not, however, consider all the facts, and what man can consider such an animal running up the trousers with equanimity – and it has happened.

The cure of such phobias is sometimes extremely difficult indeed without a complete and prolonged psychoanalysis to discover the deep associations concerned. Many are so deep, so fixed and so difficult to eradicate that in psychological parlance they are known as fixations. Fortunately many do not interfere sufficiently with the life of the individual to justify the time spent in prolonged investigation. Much can be done by argument, cajoling, ridicule, imitation and encouragement to the effect "that surely you can do what Mr. Smith can do".

Stage-fright, fear of public speaking and tongue-tiedness is extremely common, and may or may not disappear with practice. The fear may, however, not necessarily reduce the efficiency of the performance, indeed as has already been stated, it may benefit it. It is well recognised that many successful games of golf have been played by individuals who have felt extremely nervous. Robert Jones, the world's greatest golfer, has recorded that he played his best golf only when he felt nervous, while Ball won the Jubilee Vase at St. Andrews when he was so nervous that his hands were seen to tremble.

All such fears are greatly benefited by advising the subject to say to himself that he is superior in knowledge of the subject or technique of the game to the majority of audience, opponents or onlookers.

There can be little doubt too, that many associations of fear can be fixed in a child by too protective parents. The child who is not allowed to play football or cricket, to climb trees or ride horses because such acts are dangerous, may never outgrow his timidity and he tends to shrink from all danger. Later he may become antisocial or his wife and family may suffer as a result, for he may be unable to face an uncomfortable journey, an essential operation or even support a good cause in the face of opposition. We frequently see, however, physical timidity associated with moral courage and the reverse as compensations. It is not intended from the above that parents should not warn their children of the danger of doing certain things for children may not otherwise know of the danger, but the probabilities must be understood.

Fear of pain is commonly, too, a factor in indigestion, the patient being quite convinced that this or that article of diet will cause certain symptoms because the symptoms occurred on some occasion when really the patient's digestion was so depressed from some other reason that any article of diet might have caused the symptoms. It is often found that such fear of certain articles of diet have no real relation to scientific probability and that other articles of similar chemical or physical constitution may not be complained of. In many cases the special article of diet is given the blame because it chanced to be associated with some other circumstance which was really responsible. As we shall see, the kindred states of worry and anxiety produced similar states.

Anxiety, which is an unreasonable fear in the sense that the circumstances which bring it about are not immediate, is dealt with in a later section since other instincts are concerned in its production. Both fear and anxiety produce the same physiological effects, namely, intense sympathetic activity or its suppression.

Obsessions–It is evident that it is but a small step from the more potent fears and phobias to the state in which the subject becomes overcome with various ideas which are known as obsessions, which may be so powerful as to affect the conduct of the patient that he has to be restrained in a lunatic asylum. These obsessions may be of a very varied kind and are commonly those of compulsion. But here again there is not necessarily a great difference between the person who says that so and so doesn't like him or hates him, and he who says that so and so wants to, indeed, has tried to murder him. Such an obsession may lead to the patient being depressed and may even cause him to murder so and so in imagined self-defence or vengeance. Psychotherapists of the Freudian school tell us that obsessions and fears may in a much less direct way depend on wishes. Thus, when an individual has a fear of poisoning someone or of suicide he may, on deep analysis, be found to wish to be rid of the someone he fears poisoning, someone, for example, who stands in the way of his ambition, or really wishes to escape life for some reason or another, or wishes to punish himself for some misdeed he has, or imagines he has, done. Actually there is a threat to his security as a result of the obsession. In the case of the fear of suicide the patient wishes to escape but fears the consequences of such a drastic step.

Minor obsessions occur in quite normal persons and accounts for acts depending on superstitions. Many persons will not readily pick up their own glove or umbrella if they let them fall. They "touch wood" if they make a boast, they throw salt over the shoulder with the opposite hand if they spill it and break spells in many other ways.

Various superstitions are based on fears, but superstitious persons are not necessarily the persons who have the latent fears. In many cases superstitions have been passed on by tradition and hearsay or some person whose opinion has been considered specially valuable in childhood.

The Response to Fear

Different people respond very differently to fear and this has been well seen in relation to air raids. From the point of view of psychological study these have been of great advantage in that they have provided a common stimulus to a great variety of persons and the different reactions seen must be considered to be due to their psychological make-up and subsequent experience.

The natural response to fear is flight and this is commonly seen in both animals and man. In a more highly evolved world, fear has by convention been despised largely because it throws the responsibility for counteracting the fear on someone else who may be all the less able to overcome the offending object without assistance. We are all aware of the unfortunate results of failure of groups of individuals to stand up to an aggressor. Sometimes the flight is quite precipitous and so unreasonable that it is an actual disadvantage as is seen typically in the panic which may occur when a erowded building goes on fire, when there has been invasion and many other terrifying circumstances. Some have an uncontrollable impulse to escape and hide in a dark place like an animal. The escape however may be mental rather than physical and this is essentially the reaction of persons who faint or get drunk in emergencies.

Another response is simple negativism. The individual simply does nothing. This is seen typically in the child who is afraid or shy, it just stands and stares, those too who take undue care. They look too long before they leap and will not climb high buildings, drive in a motor-car, fly in an aeroplane, sit in the front coach of a train, and so on although the danger is negligible. In more acute circumstances the individual remains "rooted to the spot". We are familiar with persons who when air raids were imminent did not do anything to protect themselves, their families or their homes but sometimes panicked when the danger became more real and blame the authorities for not doing something. It was as if they put the disagreeable idea of bombing out of their minds.

This as we shall see in a later section may have been in part quite an unconscious repression.

In some cases the individuals believe like some children that they cannot come to harm and others even have a guilt complex which leads them to think that they not only do not deserve to escape but that they will certainly be hurt. These considerations are no doubt at the root of the fatalism of many persons who simply believe that "if their name is not on" a particular shell or bomb they will not get hurt. The chance is then looked upon as being somewhat similar to winning a Derby Sweepstake, and less than that of cutting an ace in ten cuts. Unfortunately in illness, such fatalism in regard to death is a disadvantage, for if the patient thinks he is going to die and does not make a fight for life, his natural defences may not be mobilised and his chances of dying may be increased.

The average person feels a sense of shame in showing fear and does what he can to combat it by employing a variety of expedients. Many are to be encouraged amongst those who are afraid. The necessity of showing a good example to others is a good antidote to fear. Often, indeed, in cases of emergency a doctor may be a source of great moral strength to the patient and his friends, although the courage and coolness may be born of a sense of duty rather than of confidence and lack of anxiety.

He may repress the fear altogether and cultivate the idea consciously and unconsciously that the danger does not exist or at least exists to such a small extent that it can be neglected. Real knowledge commonly shows this to be true, for example, it can indeed be calculated by simple arithmetic that the chances of death from an air raid in London are less than those of driving from London to Brighton ten times on a Saturday in the summer.

He may deliberately do something to take the attention from the danger. This commonly takes the form of caring for someone else but much less useful expedients such as games or reading may suffice. The doing of something really useful is however best. Of special value in preventing fear after an accident is to do the dangerous action again in safety. This is encouraged amongst airmen and racing motorists after a crash for it has been found that if this is not done an undue nervousness of the activity is liable to develop.

Sometimes there is an excessive over-compensation of the fear which results in such complete neglect of the danger that it amounts to bravado or showing off of the absence of fear without any adequate reason. Often, however, as we shall see, the normal compensation leads to real courage.

Courage and Bravery

This may be defined as the doing of an action with the full knowledge of the dangers which are involved and in cold blood. It is essentially a reaction to duty, to the herd and to spiritual values. A man may believe the cause in which he is acting is much greater than his own life, and this is the attitude which has from earliest times been encouraged in war-time and is embodied in the exhortation. "Dulce et decorum est pro patria mori". In many races it is held that this is the most noble way of dying. In other cases "the perfect love casteth out fear". In many cases, however, these considerations do not come into the picture at the moment of the danger. Those who have "gone over the top" in the face of artillery fire tell us that the excitement and exhilaration of the moment completely obliterates the sense of fear which may have been present when the action was contemplated.

The courage which is the result of prolonged fear and anxiety is dealt with in relation to anxiety which is quite as real as fear but there may in fact be no immediate danger.

Anger and Rage

The emotion of anger is aroused when there is frustration of an instinct or urge which is temporarily at least more important in the mind than that of personal security. The stimulus may be a threat to security itself either of the individual or those in whom he may have a special interest and it is most effective when acute. These facts show themselves in a variety of expressions in common use, such as "even a worm will turn", "it made him see red", "stung into response". In law too we have the judgment of homicide as distinct from murder which is previously contemplated homicide, in France there is the "unwritten law", while often a man when he realises the true implication of his act and the threat to his security which it may involve, expresses sorrow at what he has said or done "in the heat of the moment".

Anger is produced most commonly when there is disparagement of the personal prestige of the individual which may become involved in a variety of ways, his honour, his self-respect, his physical or mental power, or the cause which he supports. There may be merely mental or verbal reaction but sometimes the reaction is more violent and there is the physical reaction of fight against the offender. Sometimes instead of venting the anger on the offender, the passion is released on some object less liable to react. Thus, there is a release of the emotion by breaking crockery or furniture. Anger is, however, essentially emotional and as such is irrational, there is no use in attempting to reason with an angry man. Because it is irrational, it is also incompletely controlled and dangerous. A similar state may be produced in animals by removal of the cerebral cortex. A cat, for example, deprived of the cerebrum, that part of the brain which normally adapts its reactions to its social environment, shows every sign of loss of that control and is described as being in a state of "sham rage". This suggests that the emotion is dependent on a release of more primitive lower centres from the higher centres which are concerned primarily with the acquired reactions which depend on experience. At a certain stage in alcoholism a similar liability to anger and truculence may occur and is indicated in the expression "fighting full".

By convention the emotion of anger is deprecated in the community because of its possibly dangerous results. Children are therefore exhorted not to lose their tempers and are often punished if they do so. It becomes evident, however, that different children even when brought up almost identically vary very much in their liability to lose their tempers. Some hold that this is inherent because of their heredity or in very early childhood but it must be admitted many children have minor experiences in infancy which may pass unnoticed by adults yet profoundly affect the child.

Loss of temper amongst adults is usually considered to be evidence that the person is suffering from an inferiority which he tries to hide or as we say a "man who gets angry shows his raw spot". Sometimes as the years go on we see persons who for one reason or another become crotchety and ill-tempered, euphemistically it is sometimes called "liverish". The classical ill-temper of the retired colonel may better be that he feels unduly the inferiority of being old and of not having retired as a general, coupled possibly by a physical inferiority of health.

Those individuals who get angry easily often choose in a most remarkable way those with whom they lose their tempers. From this it is usually assumed that they are fundamentally cowards. This is a matter for debate for a similar state is seen in animals, a cat or a rat will seldom attack a man but may very courageously attack a dog. A lion or a bull too may attack one man but not another.

The liability to get angry is not a constant factor. In the animal world we see animals who become extremely ferocious in protecting their young although they may be most friendly at other times. It would seem therefore that periodic variations in the relative importance of the instincts occur and it is not improbable that this may subsequently be related to other hormonal influences associated with reproduction.

4

THE SEX INSTINCT

It is in regard to this instinct that modern psychology is most difficult to those beginning the subject for in the theory of Freud there are included, under the term sex, many activities which are not normally considered so in ordinary parlance.

The instinct to reproduce is so universal in all biology that it may be considered a fundamental characteristic of life itself, for without it life cannot continue. In a civilised life food and protection are so commonly assured, and sexual gratification so limited that problems of sex assume a special importance, the more so as it is also given a special importance in certain religious and social teachings.

In animals the instinct of sex is seen in the desire for companionship with the opposite sex, the desire to perform the sexual act, reproduction and the protection of the young. In man, however, all stages are not seen and for various reasons, which are discussed later, development may cease at any of these stages.

Sexual maturity in man commences at puberty, a period during which considerable physical changes take place. In the female the periodic ovulation and menstrual flow from the uterus commences, hair appears on the pubis and the breasts enlarge, in the male the voice changes, there is a growth of public hair and the testis produce spermatozoa.

The mental changes, which denote the awakening of the instinct, do not occur so suddenly and there is a considerable variation in different persons. Some do not appear to have the instinct awakened until later and some never at all. In most, however, the period of adolescence commences with what has been described as a "homosexual" phase in which there is a desire for the companionship of the same sex. There is an attraction to elders of the same sex. How far this is fundamental and how far it is an accidental result of conditions of education is difficult to determine. Some hold that it is less seen in co-education schools where the sexes meet as is common in the country as distinct from towns. Those who consider this stage fundamental emphasise that this period depends on the fact that male and female elements and hormones are not yet distinct. While, however, it is true that anatomical elements, both male and female, are present in the adult, their differentiation is normally fully marked at puberty if it is going to occur at all. It may be that hormonal differentiation is not complete, that is, it is possible that certain cells in the pituitary, adrenal cortex or gonads which influence mental sexual differentiation are not complete. This is suggested by the common occurrence in females at this stage of hair on the upper lip which subsequently disappears. During the period of adolescence it would seem that the bond of union between the individuals of the same sex is natural curiosity regarding life in general and sex in particular. The generative organs hitherto have been considered solely in relation to excretion. The adolescent finds it almost impossible to comprehend a large amount of what is going on in the world without a knowledge of sex, for literature, the play, the cinema, and the news of the day abound with allusions to its power and its interest to adults.

It is the satisfaction of the sex instinct which presents the great psychological problem, for it is obvious that, for many reasons, this is not always possible because of social and economic considerations at an age when the urge is at its strongest and fertility at its highest. The problem is greater in regard to women, for most have the misfortune not only to be born into a monogamous world, but a world in which, for various reasons, more females survive to adult life than males. War accentuates the difference. The subject is discussed further in relation to the "The Instinct of Herd".

Nor is the instinct satisfied by marriage for one of the partners may, for some reason, be deficient in some respect. To a woman, however, marriage means more than to a man. Until achieved it may take up the major portion of a woman's thoughts and for many it is the sole achievement desired largely because of the security it affords. It also satisfies their power urge. For men and women with careers it plays a less important part, although even for the latter it often offers overwhelming attraction if we judge from the number of successful women who exchange their professions for domesticity.

Fortunately for those to whom fate has been less kind, nature provides compensation and mental processes by which there is some appeasement of their instincts.

When the security instincts are endangered the reproductive instinct is not only stimulated but special care is taken of the offspring, the protection of which becomes even more important than the protection of the self. Many animals defend their young to the death, while human communities protect "women and children first". It may be that this is because they are weaker, but it may be part of a more general biological urge. Even plants when their survival is threatened, flower and seed more freely than if grown under more kindly conditions, while even bacteria produce spores which have a better chance of survival than the parent.

Infantile Relations with Parents

It is on this subject that opinions regarding modern psychology are most sharply divided. On the one hand, there are the followers of Freud who consider these relationships as essentially sexual and that this "infantile sexuality" has a profound effect on adult life. On the other hand, there are others who prefer to take these relationships at their face value. The facts are not disputed.

A child from the time it is born is usually largely dependent for food and protection on its mother or some other female taking her place. If breast fed it takes particular interest in the breast and nipple. The other activities in which a special interest is taken are its excretions. It is exhorted to excrete at certain times and if complacent in this respect it may receive certain pleasurable marks of approval. The pleasures of the infant and its first regular contact with the outside world are those of feeding and excretion. Freudians describe them as oral and anal eroticisms. There is, however, a striking absence of evidence of any generally recognised differences between breast-fed and bottle-fed babies, although no doubt differences might be claimed!

Gradually the child becomes aware of a world other than itself and learns that it may attract attention by crying. The value it puts on crying depends on the response of the parents, and like any animal it learns rapidly (if properly trained) the uselessness of crying when it requires nothing but social attention. Some claim to recognise too a mental strain produced by a too sudden weaning.

Freudians attribute finger-sucking to oral eroticism and trace with remarkable ingenuity an interest from the pleasures of excretions, to playing with excreta and later the playing of the adult with coins in the pocket. They also consider that by manipulation of the genitals, children obtain pleasurable sensations which they call infantile masturbation. There is, however, little real evidence that the response is anything more than a simple response to the local irritation which is so common in this region.

Mother and Father, hate or love – It is well recognised that in adolescent and adult life there is a tendency for love between son and mother while there may be antagonism between son and father. On the other hand, there may be attraction between daughter and father, while there may be antagonism to the mother. There is several possible explanations of this. Freud drew attention to what he called the Œdipus Complex. The name is based on the Greek tragedy of Sophocles in which Œdipus is caused by the Fates unknowingly to kill his father and subsequently to marry his mother, but when he finds out what he has done he puts out his own eyes. There is a similar ancient story of Electra who assisted in the slaying of her mother. It is considered that the child sees in the father an object capable of taking away the mother and who is a rival in the mother's affections. Thus is developed, it is thought, a fundamental antagonism of a son to a male parent. The application of the story of Electra, which is claimed to account for mother-daughter antagonism, is still more fanciful, but such situations are accepted by many leading psychologists as a background of mental illness.

It would seem just as reasonable to consider that the antagonism arises later when the mother, naturally more concerned with the upbringing of the daughter, who may chafe under authority as the son may do under that of a father whose duty it becomes to exhort him in the pursuit of a life work according to his lights which may not be those of the son, for it will be generally admitted (although this is commonly ignored by psychologists) that the mother hate is by no means a universal feeling of daughters any more than father hate is universal amongst men. It is worthy of note that in the animal world parental and filial affection is very short lived. Amongst intelligent breeds of dogs, female parents and offsprings appear to forget each other entirely after a few months' separation, indeed, a dog remembers more readily its human master than its parent. It would therefore be quite logical to consider father-son antagonism to be due to a lack of development of affection rather than a new development of antagonism.

Whatever the cause of antagonisms when they exist, it is certainly wise for the parent to be made aware of the liability of their occurrence and to prevent it by arranging as far as possible, for any necessary admonition to be given by the opposite sex.

Psychologists claim that daughters who are father-lovers tend to marry men much older than themselves and thus secure parental security, while sons who are mother-lovers tend to marry older women or women whom they expect to act as mothers than as wives. Where the mother has "spoiled" the son and devoted undue attention to his wishes great difficulty may arise, especially when the wife has to give much of her time to the care of children.

Parental Domination – The fact that parents may completely fail to recognise that their children have grown up often leads to difficult situations and mental distress to all concerned. The state would appear to arise from an exaggeration of the parental instinct, especially in the absence of any other interest to replace it, and where the children have continued to live at home too long. It may, however, give satisfaction of the power urge in the absence of any other. The disastrous effects of such states are seen in the lack of confidence of the children who continually look to the parents for guidance feeling that they are always right although the parents may be quite unable to give good advice.

5

THE URGE FOR POWER

The desire for power is in a sense secondary to the instincts, but in the human species is so important that it requires special consideration. In all colonies of animals we see that certain animals assert their superiority. If animals are observed feeding it is commonly seen that some will stand aside and give preference to others. Wild geese or ducks fly in formation obviously with a leader.

The sense of competition in play is, however, developed at a very early age in animals as well as man. Young lambs are commonly seen to compete with each other in running to the top of a hill, or chickens will race to be fed presumably because the first gets most.

It would seem that in the main this power, when achieved, is derived from a physical superiority which would confer preference in regard to protection, food supply and sexual relations and therefore confers security on the individual and his family. In the animal world where the rule of force prevails, this is of special importance. In many primitive human societies where individuals assume leadership because of their physical superiority, a relic of which persists in schools where the school captain is chosen because of his prowess at games and thereby secures certain definite privileges and is the ideal of the small boys. Later, a man may owe his success even in a mental sphere more to a physical appearance of power than to his mental capability, or as we say "he looks the part". Often in the academic or professional sphere there is such reluctance to admit mental superiority of another that physical superiority gains the distinction just as in instances of physical demand, as in revolutions, men of meagre stature may become leaders. Vying with the school captain, however, is the dux who becomes so because of mental superiority.

In adult societies of the modern world, in which we see the influence of the power urge very markedly, leaders are chosen in similar ways but other less desirable features, factors such as assertiveness and appeal to average desires are also important. Some leaders do not lead but are facile at interpreting desire. Sometimes the leader chosen depends on the nature of the occasion and his capability of doing what is needed.

The power urge may be looked upon as partly inherited and partly acquired, as it is certainly present in very different degrees in different persons although usually absence in one direction is compensated for by urge in another. It has been described as possessed of energy which must gain expression, and if it does not obtain this in one way it will if it has sufficient energy do so in another. In a few persons only is it absent altogether. Very commonly activity in a certain direction is induced by ambitious parents who direct the early thoughts.

The power urge shows itself in several different forms. In youth the satisfaction is obtained through sport, or educational activity, but ambition and money-making are perhaps the commonest in adults. The desire to possess, or to make, or to have power over others are also well recognised, but there are many others which often pass unrecognised.

It is well recognised that failure to achieve success may lead to illness. This, we shall see in a later section, is most commonly an escape, since the illness suggests that the patient has been overworking and may be considered by the patient as an excuse for his failure, and thus he escapes any aspersions against his failure whether they be real or imagined. Illness, however, may have a direct relation to the power urge and is most commonly seen in regard to patients who succeed in establishing power and control over those whose "duty" it is to look after them. Thus, a parent may succeed in completely dominating and indeed ruining the life of a son or daughter. They may demand that the daughter is essential to look after the mother or the house, or that the son is needed to assist in the family business. Too often the parent slacks off work and the life of the son or daughter becomes circumscribed and impoverished as a result of what is little more than a form of selfishness which, however, is tolerated by the community. Such parents have to be exhorted to think of their children's future, at least equally with their own comfort.

Usually the urge for power is demonstrative. The acquired title, rich house, expensive motor-car or other possessions in England, the expensive mistress in France, the richly dressed woman in America all bespeak the success, money and the power of the man concerned. Such phenomena are not, however, confined to human beings and is well seen in the obvious strutting of the turkey cock or the peacock in full plumage even in the absence of admirers of their own species.

In the case of the woman, rich dress, jewels and successful family play their part in providing elation and it is often quite pathetic to see the extent to which parents, especially women, will sacrifice themselves to satisfy their power urge through the success of their children. The notorious "cattiness" and anti-social tendencies of women is probably a related phenomenon through which women, especially the childless and unmarried, assert their power urge over their more successful sisters.

The satisfaction of the power urge is, however not always harmful, indeed, it may be fairly said that it is commonly the urge which makes men and women "do things" in their own special sphere. Often a man prefers to be somebody in a small sphere than a nobody in a larger sphere. This preference to be a large frog in a small pond to being a small frog in a large pond often prevents men from moving from the provinces to London and for men preferring life in provincial communities. Every community has its busy-bodies which satisfy their power urge. Some professions tend to attract such persons, notably the teaching profession and the church. In common parlance when we say that a man has been a school-teacher we at once excuse him for his tendency to be boring, dogmatic and excessively opinionated. In the latter case we commonly see what was possibly, in the first instance, a spiritual urge, becoming more and more one of power circumscribed though it is. Some men translate through the medium of money one form of power into another. This we commonly see in the purchase of unnecessary possessions or the thinly disguised purchase of a title. The possessions may be chosen to suggest power in other directions as is common in the purchase of books or art objects. Greed is merely this desire for possession carried to excess and to an extent which causes the deprivation of others. It is a vice in so far as it is anti-social, but it is a perfectly natural animal urge.

It is this urge too which drives on adventurous spirits to fresh endeavour and new discoveries which are for the benefit of mankind. That is, however, not to say that all endeavour and discovery depend on the power urge, for men continue to strive from other motives.

Fortunately for those who desire it there is some power satisfaction of some kind for almost everybody in the world, but occasionally it takes strange forms. Thus, a man who is bullied at business secures satisfaction by bullying those unfortunates over whom he has control, his assistants, his family or those who may have to wait on him at meal-time especially those in restaurants who cannot retaliate by giving "notice". More commonly when a man fails to find satisfaction in one outlet he escapes to another sphere of activity and tries another. Thus, a man dissatisfied in academic life may turn administrator or even politician, a fact no doubt which contributes to notoriously inefficient administration and bureaucratic bullying.

The frustration of the power urge leads to such intensely important and undesirable emotions as hate, envy, jealousy, which do much to destroy human happiness, and to the feeling of inferiority which may lead to much melancholy and despair. The circumstances which may lead to the frustration are very varied, and the reactions produced are not always so unfortunate as the evil emotions just mentioned suggest. Indeed, there may result such valuable qualities as valour, patience and perseverance.

The constructive instinct is closely related to the power instinct and there can be no doubt that there are many people who derive their greatest pleasure out of "making something". It may be building up a business or an institution, making something with the hands, writing books. It is so much commoner to find the destructive critic who destroys that made by others, largely because it is made by others, and put nothing else in its place. "The new broom sweeps clean but sweeps empty".

Unfortunately the constructive instinct does not run parallel with ability or perseverance, otherwise we should not find so many half-finished tasks in the world. We are always meeting those individuals who "intend to do things" but never do. "I always mean to" they will say and may even begin but never finish, usually because they are too lazy. How often we see in research an individual who commences a piece of research but never finishes it, yet feels grieved if it is suggested that somebody else might.

It is the satisfaction of the power and constructive instincts which is the basis of the well-known adage that nothing is more satisfying than a job well done.

The failure to satisfy this urge is one of the commonest causes of illness in modern civilisation and in all classes of society.

The Rôle of Money – In a civilised society money plays a very important rôle in the provision of the necessaries of a physical and mental life. Money is essentially a substitute for more cumbersome possessions, and for labour into which it may be converted. With it we purchase food but it must be realised that theoretically we exchange the labour which provides the money for the labour of the individuals who physically wrest the food from nature. We tend to forget that someone must catch and kill the animals we eat, dig our potatoes or harvest our wheat.

It seems probable that the accumulation of possessions is human weakness which is closely allied, if not merely a highly civilised adaptation of the animal instinct, to hoard food as the dog buries its bones or the squirrel collects nuts. The characteristic is indeed common amongst animals and is an instinct to provide for periods when the things hoarded will not be so easily available. Where the possession is ostentatious it is, however, closely related to vanity.

Money also provides security. By the taxes we pay there is kept up the civil forces of law and order. Admittedly, however, in a completely and really civilised community this would not be necessary. In providing this security, however, we are at the same time depriving ourselves of the natural instinct to provide it directly, we may indeed forget its necessity until war is upon us. We may, however, in peace, purchase substitutes which satisfy this instinct, by attending shows or films of events involving competition, adventure, danger to others, or by taking part in sports or competitive games, and commonly it is found that such spectacles are attended by those whose lives are most secure.

Money may also purchase substitutes for normal sex life, but more commonly it purchases substitutes in the form of love stories portrayed by film or book. In the childless it may make possible the adoption of children, the keeping of animals, the running of welfare homes and a thousand other activities.

Money also, in the less civilised portion of society, which is unfortunately its largest portion and independent of social status, confers a considerable amount of power on its possessor and thus satisfies his vanity although the power and the vanity may remain latent as in the case of the miser. Money often provides, amongst business men, the sole means by which they can demonstrate their ability and success in business. The large house and motor-car have become almost acknowledged evidence of success that many purchase them as spurious evidence of such success when they can ill afford them. The necessity for a certain expensive and often uncomfortable address is, in many quarters, looked upon as essential not only for business, but for social acceptance amongst those of similar mentality. There are, moreover, sufficient who accept such criteria to make it worthwhile for doctors to maintain appearances they can often ill afford. From the more strictly medical point of view is must, however, be kept in mind that the acquisition of money is, to a vast number of persons, a measure of success and thereby contributes to health in those who have no other measure. In such persons its absence may produce misery and ill-health.

Money can also purchase escape and this is a very important consideration in a civilised world of a reality which for many is stark and hard. By the purchase of amusement and diversion of different kinds the individual, if he cannot think, merely escapes into a world where thought is unnecessary, and if he thinks, escapes from the knowledge of the futility and vanity of much human endeavour, especially his own. Or it may be he escapes from a world of dull monotony into a world of excitement, adventure and romance. In so far as it does purchase escape, money may produce a spurious variety of content. It cannot, however, buy the things most worth having to those who think, such as affection, health and happiness, although it may bring them nearer. There is no evidence that the rich, or well-to-do, are any happier than the poor, and as many commit suicide. When then we say that money in excess of what is needed to provide the necessaries of life and a few luxuries merely satisfies a primitive power urge, it is probably correct.

6

THE INSTINCT OF HERD

It is well recognised that certain animals tend to group themselves into herds. This characteristic is seen amongst certain birds, insects, sheep and wolves, and there seems little doubt that it is concerned with protection as in the case of sheep, or power as in the case of wolves. This instinct is, as it were, part of the beast itself. It resists separation and may often be observed as in the case of warning against an enemy, to feel a primary responsibility to the herd which may take precedence over its own protection.

Many students of this subject hold that man is similarly essentially a gregarious animal. He tends to dwell in communities, he is sensitive to the voice of the herd, the passion of the pack, attracted by warmth, susceptible to leadership and intolerant of solitude, mental or physical, in regard to himself or the activities of others. The importance of this characteristic has been emphasised especially by Trotter who in his *Instinct of the Herd* has shown how potent this herd influence may be in determining the reactions not only of individuals but of nations.

Whether we subscribe to the view or not, that gregariousness and all that it entails is an inherent and important characteristic of man, there can be no doubt that practically all normal individuals obey the dictates of the community in which they live to an extent which is seldom appreciated. It may be that it is due to our early training, to our natural power of imitation, or to the realisation that it is for the most part in our interests to do so, but certainly it is developed at an early age for schoolchildren are even more intolerant of divergence of standards than adults. In all communities we find however, the "lone sheep" or "lone wolf".

In all communities, but especially in a modern civilised world, there is a tendency to submit inevitably to certain conventions and restraints. These we see in regard to the primary instincts, Protection, Food and Sex. The conventions of the community are well seen in relation to clothes. Both sexes submit to a fashion which has become a tyranny, and in the case of women the tyranny increases with the purse. But even men do not arrive at the University or at business on a hot day dressed in shorts and shirts only, although admittedly there is no justifiable reason why they do not do so. The clothes convention in regard to morning dress has indeed become so international that its adoption has become a conventional indication of civilised emancipation, while in regard to bathing-costumes conventional emancipation is indicated by approximation to that of the South Sea Islander.

Chivalry in its medieval sense has passed. Fighting is a "breach of the peace", but we still are allowed to protect ourselves or our country by use of force, even to the extent of killing the enemy; indeed, we are expected to do so.

A convention which is of the greatest importance in medicine is that by which the sick or the wounded are considered deserving of sympathy and a demand upon the resources of the community. As a result of this, vast and increasing numbers of doctors are kept in employment at public expense and a vast number of persons are kept alive who would otherwise succumb to the natural law of the survival of the fittest. The origin of the convention is obscure but it is probably multiple. From earliest times sympathy for the sick has been shown and this has been the great function of the Church throughout the ages as part of the teaching of Christ epitomised in the story of the good samaritan. The treatment of sick prisoners of war equally with our own casualties is probably a survival of the days of chivalry passed on to us by the Order of St. John. It finds expression also in the code that we do not strike a man when he is down. The whole idea is probably a robust demonstration of the power urge which suggests that although our enemy may rise to fight another day we can again beat him, combined again with the teaching of Christ in the sermon on the mount, that we should love our enemies. The latter exhortation is itself good psychology in that by so doing a state of mental rest is produced. There is little doubt too, that in purely secular communities free medical treatment represents psychologically an attempt of the community to accept and at the same time atone for the disgrace of the existence of the sick poor which are thereby escaped. At the same time it will be realised that the community is quite illogical in that it breaks the natural law by promoting the survival of the unfit without at the same time insisting on any appreciable standard of health, for it is admitted on all sides that our hospitals are thronged with preventable diseases which are the direct result of that fantastic delusion that uneducated man is capable of controlling his own health in a modern world. That sooner or later we shall see compulsory medical inspection of the whole community, in its own interest, is without doubt. In higher forms of civilisation the weak, whether they be individuals or nations, are protected. While instead of the natural law of the survival of the fittest we see, in war, their fantastic destruction in the interest of the weak and the survival of the unfit.

Our play, too, has become conventionalised by the introduction of certain fixed games with rules and it is expected that Britons "will play the game" as truly as they did in the days of chivalry. They will not hit an enemy when he is down, they will respect the courage in a beaten adversary as was done in the coliseum of ancient Rome.

In regard to food we have conventional methods adapted to certain circumstances in regard to articles of food, order of eating them and utensils employed. The conventions are not, however, identical in all countries, and slow changes are seen. Thus, we have seen liver, since it has become of medicinal value and expensive, become an article of diet of the well-to-do when before it was despised. We take fish before meat, and it is no longer taboo to take luncheon on a high stool at a counter. It is even more than a convention that there are ideals worth living for dearer than even life itself.

In relation to sex we see a host of conventions many of which are biologically sound and not a few are futile.

In most communities the stronger man is expected to defend the weaker women and children. In a shipwreck women and children are first. In danger of air raids children are evacuated to safety. It will be realised that such conventions are essentially to ensure the continuance of the species and is not confined to humans.

Reproduction is permitted according to very definite rules designed for the most part to ensure economic protection of children and old women, although nothing is done to prevent the reproduction of the unfit whose progeny become a burden to the community.

Healthy unmarried women are not permitted to bear children but are allowed to adopt and lavish maternal kindness on animals or human beings of which they are not the parents, if they can afford to do so. This rule tends to be enforced especially by the older married women who thereby reduce competition.

There are, however, very great variations in different communities in taste, reticence, modesty and morality towards sex, and the effect on the child mind must also vary very much.

Even instruction in sex has until recent years been ignored. Many parents found it difficult if not actually indecent, to instruct their children in regard to the process of mammalian propagation. This is based on a conventional idea that discussion of all parts of the body related to those of excretion are unclean and to be kept hidden from view and from thoughts. The convention is not universal, mixed bathing in the nude is the mode in certain Baltic countries. The covering of the nipples is not considered necessary in males, nor by females in some countries. In some special liberty is allowed when a child must be fed.

It will be realised that the conventions of the herd to which we are attached for the time being may be quite different from the herd in other places. We say that "when in Rome we do as the Romans do", that a man is a good mixer or is very adaptable when he can adjust his reactions to the company in which he chances to find himself. Not only so, but when we revisit a place after an absence of years we realise that in the meantime local habits may have changed quite appreciably.

The world is indeed composed of a vast number of little communities each within the other and overlapping considerably. What is "bad form" or "not done" in one is allowed or "O.K." in another. Each community has its leaders and its conventions, and each community judges the social status of individuals and their reactions in certain environments. In the less civilised but moneyed world, using the term in its highest sense, capability of following the fashion of the month "oft proclaims the man"—more commonly the woman.

On the whole, however, the rules of the community in so far as they promote health and happiness, are for the benefit of the community, although they may bring hardship to individuals and especially the young who often chafe under their restraints, for in a civilised world restraint is what obedience to the herd means in practice. There are, however, few who do not feel the restraint in some form or other. Fortunately much has been so fixed in us in our early days that the reactions involved are almost automatic. We find ourselves apologizing to strangers who bump into us in the street, although in fact we may not have been to Mame, and so on with the thousands of little reactions which have become part of ourselves.

With the advance of civilisation we no longer tolerate rule by physical force, but we must understand that this reaction in civilisation is quite recent and is not adhered to by many nations who consider themselves civilised because they have access to, and utilise modern inventions. There is little doubt that rule by force is, however, the only method of rule in the case of animals, of certain children and of certain nations. In their immaturity they understand no other and mistake the absence of force as weakness, while many amongst us, especially since 1918, fondly imagined that it was possible to inculcate the convention of our community by kindness only, but the last ten years has provided the world with sufficient individuals and nations to prove the futility of attempting to flout what are simple biological laws.

As we grow older we try to inculcate social laws into those over whom we have control and tend to become more and more intolerant of change. It is quite remarkable indeed how men who have themselves contributed quite materially to scientific knowledge, tend to be intolerant of evidence which contradicts their established views—and especially when the new knowledge has been discovered by someone who chances not to belong to their own little herd. This is often ascribed to "old school tie" or pride of University etc. etc., but those who take the broader biological view merely see the simple reaction of the gregarious animal outcropping as it were through the civilised crust.

In what has been said above, the view has been taken that the responses are essentially those of the herd. It must however be understood that it would be quite as justifiable to consider many of them as adaptations to environment for in most cases we can recall the process of having learnt them. It is not possible to distinguish clearly between what reactions are essentially due to our gregarious instinct and what are the result of experience. We see a very large number of similar reactions in domestic animals. These reactions which are the result of experience are for all practical purposes conditioned reflexes like the tricks we may teach our pet dog.

It is seen that the impelling forces of the environment or of the herd, are ever with us and run counter to those of the primary instinct concerned in nutrition, self-preservation and reproduction. The forces of the former usually gain ascendency in the abstract. This is true in regard to the control of others. For the individual concerned it is quite another matter when he is faced with starvation, prospect of physical hurt or death and the emotions involved in sex. He may find himself quite unable to obey the dictates of the herd and be overcome by the emotion or he may develop a state of conflict or frustration (this is discussed in a subsequent section).

Special Inhibitions Leading to Abnormal Adult Reactions – Some of the inhibitions imposed by the community, or by that part of the community which is responsible for our early upbringing, are developed so strongly that they cannot readily be released even when the inhibitions are no longer desired. These are commonly concerned with the excretions and sex.

Micturition and Defaecation – As pointed out by Pavlov, micturition is an excellent example of the establishment of a conditioned reflex overcoming a natural act. At an early age we have been taught that the urinary bladder should be emptied only at certain times and places. Many boys have great difficulty in commencing the act in public urinals and very few persons could probably do so on a public platform. Many have difficulty of micturition when confined to bed, and various devices such as pouring out water or moving the hands in water are used to facilitate the act. Similar difficulty in defaecating in bed is common, or publicly in the multiple latrines used in war-time. The fact that in the house-trained young dog there is a conditioned inhibition in relation to micturition is shown by the effect of excitement which may release the inhibition.

Sexual Impotence – There is little doubt that many cases of inability to perform the sexual act is in the same category. As a result of being brought up with the idea that all matters concerning the sexual organs are unclean, the whole sexual act may become so inhibited, or the idea so repugnant, that in the male erection does not occur, or there may be sexual anæsthesia in either the male or female. It is not suggested, however, that all cases of sexual impotence of psychic origin are necessarily produced in the same way.

Imitation – A feature of the herd instinct is imitation. When we join a new herd we try to become part of it, for in so doing we become secure of position and safe. Here again it becomes evident that the animal by imitation takes advantage of the experience of another. Sheep follow "like sheep", but in many spheres of life we see imitations. The young surgeon tends to imitate his teachers, the young artist tends to follow the methods of his masters and often this remains evident in his later work. The young housewife does things like her mother, indeed it may be fairly said that an enormous amount of human endeavour is based on imitation whether it be clothes, work or play. Even suicides tend to imitate each other. Imitation is also seen amongst hysterical patients who may acquire normal movements.

Socially, imitation makes us safe with herd – imitation is not only the sincerest form of flattery but is also etiquette – whether it be in regard to clothes, customs or manners.

By imitation the individual takes advantage of the experience of others and cannot therefore be blamed when things go wrong. It is for this reason that we see fashion even in medicine. Many quite good therapeutic measures become discarded and others not any better take their place, and unfortunately the circumstances which set the fashions are often not more rational than those which dictate the fashion in ladies' clothes.

The Herd Instinct and Nutrition – The influence of herd instinct in relation to nutrition is well seen in the prevailing fashions regarding articles of diet and fashions of eating, but visits to other countries rapidly make us realise how restricted are our fashions to our own community. It is quite common for the dietetic fashion of a community to interfere with its nutrition. This is seen in the extensive use of white flour which on all sides is less wholesome than wholemeal flour, which, however, is not fashionable and more difficult and expensive to obtain, although in fact it ought to be cheaper.

The Herd Instinct and Protection – In relation to personal protection we have many examples of the operation of the herd instinct. In war the individual is frequently torn between his desire to protect himself and his sense of duty towards his country and many intense mental conflicts arise, the more so, since in a modern war in which the enemy may be so distant that he belongs almost to a land of unreality.

The Herd Instinct and Reality – Many of the emotions of life although they are based on the instincts may be so altered in context that they belong almost to a land of phantasy. The power urge or the sex instinct may entice an individual to spend his money in, or attempting to attain, some object which may in fact be so out of reach that it belongs to phantasy. The laws of the community, however, bring the dreamer back to earth in the form of creditors. Thus, obedience to the herd almost necessarily means facing reality, for the community in which we live is part of our reality in which we live.

7

FRUSTRATION AND CONFLICT

Conflict and frustration are common experiences in a civilised world. They occur when any particular emotion would cause us to respond in a certain way but for some reason the natural response is not possible. By far the commonest conflict is that in which there is incompatibility between the instinct of the herd or the rules of society and the other instincts. There are few of us who at one time or other have not felt the desire to do some of the things which are "not done". Sometimes individuals are physically or mentally incapable of carrying out their emotional desire and see not way of ever being able to do so. A man finds himself incapable of being the success in a particular sphere of life which he has chosen, a woman finds that she cannot have children. In many cases the sense of frustration may be accentuated by the attending circumstances such as the taunts of friends and relations and the sight of her neighbour's children.

This is as true politically as it is for the individuals. Small communities may, for example, retain their enmities against a neighbour long after the cause of the enmity has been righted.

Patients consult a doctor in various stages of their conflicts. They may come to him because of illness which is really due to a dysfunction of organs which has been initiated from psychological causes but may have resulted in pathological changes, and here it may be said that the success of a practitioner depends very largely on his appreciation of the conflicts of his patients and his capability of assisting their resolutions. The patients may also come, or be brought, to him because the illness is really mental and not associated with pathological change or dysfunction other than that of the nervous system. In the past these have been described as "functional" but it must be realised that from the patients point of view, they are real illnesses which may lead to permanent disability if not to a lunatic asylum.

The conflicts themselves may not be direct but may involve associations. Thus, a motorist who has fallen foul of a certain policeman may dislike policemen in general, while there are certain magistrates and policemen who appear to dislike motorists in general. A Cambridge man frustrated by an Oxford man may hate all Oxford men. The reverse however may occur! An Englishman who chances to have a good German friend may refuse to believe ill of any German. Nor are all Welshmen thieves as the story of Taffy might suggest. These association phenomena are sometimes called *displacement*.

Where an exaggerated instinct of self-preservation conflicts with the herd instinct of patriotism, the individual may become not only a conscientious objector, but an ardent pacifist and internationalist.

Conflicts occur between nations, groups of persons such as political parties, individuals and emotions. Hitherto it has been common to consider only the psychology of the individual but it must be realised that the same principles apply to all categories of persons between whom conflict may occur and all utilise the same mental mechanisms, although in some cases modified – especially by the effects of individuals upon each other.

Similar conflicts are seen between animals and between man and animals. The animal, such as a dog or a horse may know and submit to its master but may not submit to another who attempts to direct its conduct. It would seem that the study of animals in association with man has not been brought sufficiently into formal psychology although in relation to certain phenomena we sometimes refer to "the brute in man". As we shall see, the response to the conflicts show very similar reactions.

Any conflict, whether it is between nations, individuals or emotions, must have certain results. One side may win and the other be beaten, or the fight may continue indefinitely. The same is true of all the plant and animal world in their conflict with nature. Nature may win and the plant or animal die, the conflict may continue and the plant or animal continue a stunted or warped existence, or the plant or animal may adapt itself to its environment and flourish. These principles determine the normal distribution of plants and animals on the world surface and become apparent if plants or animals are moved to a new environment. The animal differs, however, from the plant in that it may be able to escape to another environment where conditions of life are more agreeable.

The mental conflicts of man result in similar reactions, there may be submission, it may be with compromise, the conflict may continue and upset the life of the individual, or there may be escape.

It is important that we should not forget the essential biological significance of the reactions. Each reaction represents a definite response of the organism to his environment. In the animal and plant world we observe the plant or animal struggling to achieve health, strength, and the latter happiness.

It is possible to study simpler instances of conflict in the "breaking" of a horse to harness or the training of a dog. There is at first intense conflict. The horse kicks and the dog is disobedient, but eventually they both learn that it is to their advantage to acquiesce and until eventually they appear to be quite happy in their acquiescence. Some submit much more readily than others, some only to certain masters but not to others, others are always difficult and are always likely "to kick over the traces". It is important to observe that submission is an inherited quality and the inheritance of difficult traits is well recognised.

We have similar differences between nations and between individuals. In some persons the conflicts resolve rapidly and easily. There are the stable, adaptable normal persons who form the bulk of society. When they submit too obviously we call them "yes men". In others, however, the conflict is longer and fiercer. They are the worriers, "the grousers", the rebels, who are in an almost constant state of resolving conflicts of one kind or another. Some of their conflicts indeed may belong almost to a world of phantasy rather than to a world of reality.

Experimental Conflict

The agitated mental state which occurs during conflict may be seen experimentally.

This is well seen in relation to the conditioned reflexes. Pavlov taught a dog that it would receive food when it was shown a circle, but no food when it was shown an oblong. When it was shown an oval the animal passed into a state of obvious mental distress similar to that found in human beings during periods of indecision.

In the nervous system there may be a conflict between two opposing reflexes. If a dog's back is scratched in the saddle area it will scratch itself with its hind leg in this region, but if another more potent stimulus is applied to another area it takes precedence and the scratch reflex is inhibited. Sherrington has shown that always the reflex which is of most importance for the survival of the animal gets precedence in the use of muscles and nerve-paths.

Types of Mental Reaction in Conflict

As has been indicated above, the types of responses may be classified biologically in accordance with the laws of logic and of nature. Commonly the mental mechanisms have not, however, been arranged in their biological perspective. In all conflicts there are three possible results:

1. Submission.
2. Escape.
3. Continuance of the conflict.

In considering this subject it will be realised that every normal person has his conflicts which he solves in his own way. The more emotional, excitable or unstable persons amongst us give exaggerated responses, but these merge insensibly with the pathological and irrational. It is now well recognised that there are many "on the fringe" of normality who, with adequate advice and treatment, may never require restraint in an asylum.

These results of conflicts have been differently interpreted by some. Others following Freud look upon these responses as being wish-fulfilment. A man who commits suicide escapes from the unhappiness of reality of life, but at the same time fulfils his wish to be at peace and in the company possibly of those already departed. Such a view tends to become fatuous in that it makes it impossible for anyone to do anything that he does not wish to do.

8

THE DESIRE FOR SUBMISSION

Submission occurs typically when a horse is broken to harness. It learns to respond to certain conventional codes imposed on it from without.

The average member of the community submits to the rules of his herd. The submission may be complete or partial. We see almost complete submission in relation to clothes which we allow to interfere very materially with our physical comfort. Even conquered nations learn to some extent that they must submit to the laws imposed by their conquerors and such nations show the same general reactions as individuals. In the present volume, however, it is the individual who concerns us.

Those who submit easily to the laws of the community never get into trouble, they are good children, law abiding citizens, good servants of the individual or of the state (in the case of civil servants). They are dull but stable members of the community, reliable and not likely to go "off the rails". If the world was governed by them progress would cease and life would have little sparkle.

We see submission in many walks of life. Even in science we see occasionally a younger man who does exactly what he is told and acts as the faithful servant to those he considers superior and by always agreeing with them may gain for himself such a completely false reputation for wisdom that it may pay to be a sychophant. Such persons are commonly not very strong personalities and go with the current of opinion and with the winning side. Sometimes however they compensate in a most remarkable way for their submission by becoming excessively "bossy" in their earnestness to secure the submission of others especially those over whom they may exercise minor control. The "officiousness" and petty tyranny of the minor official is notorious. Their "meekness" in the presence of those in authority is equally often seen.

Those who are not in positions of authority are often non-realists and have a tendency to find enjoyment in pursuits with an abstract basis such as religion, philosophy and art. They are given to good works or recreations and hobbies which do not obtrude. These are very common with those with very routine occupations. They often provide the mystics and become marked introverts. Their first thought is to obey. Real thought is no longer necessary. Physical and mental comfort is assured and there is content. There is little doubt that it is the desire for peace which leads to most submissions. It is often so much trouble to do other than submit. Some individual in authority may annoy us but it would be such a waste of time and energy to argue or take legal proceedings, that we submit. It is probably this somewhat lazy attitude which results in so many individuals ceasing to do research. It takes too much time, patience and money, and energy. There are, too, pseudo-scientists to be found in every scientific department who teach much dogma unquestioningly just as there are students who prefer to read books which contain it. It is so much easier not to question the facts as written than to be a searcher after the truth and lose a certain peace of mind. But has the poet not written –

> What is this life if, full of care,
> We have no time to stand and stare?

In states of physical exhaustion submission occurs more readily than in health. This is the basis of third degree interrogation by certain police. Even distinguished physicians or surgeons, when seriously ill, will readily succumb to an authoritative practitioner of reasonable sagacity although they might think little of his opinion in their healthier moments.

Submission occurs in many varieties which differ only in detail. Some are just too weak to say no, others are beaten into submission. The average person will submit to considerable discomfort and restraint and often does so if he thinks that they are only temporary and are for his prolonged benefit. He will submit to rationing or to a surgical operation. Commonly he limits his food and drink according to his purse.

Occasionally we see individuals whose spirit is broken and is so weak that they can scarcely defend their own rights. Such persons and nations are easily driven. This is admittedly one of the causes of shyness, but it may sometimes lead to intense depression. Some nations are less readily cowed in this way than others. Their spirit is never broken although they may be beaten.

It is interesting to observe that certain mechanisms of the nervous system tend to bring about submission. This is seen physiologically in the fact that sustained stimuli cease to stimulate by a process of adaptation at the nerve endings. The tick of the clock is not noticed, the hot bath ceases to be hot more rapidly than it gets cold. We all become accustomed to many things in life which at first were irritating.

It is in fact quite remarkable the extent to which the average human being does submit to a host of trivial restrictions imposed on him not only from without but also from within. Possibly the most outstanding is the tyranny of fashion which is imposed in a subtle way from without in order to promote trade.

It must be understood that various types of submission, especially those to the community, become so automatic that we do not recognise the restraint, indeed, the normal response is that of restraint. The restraint has instituted conditioned reflexes which it is very difficult to overcome. One of the most striking and important in medicine is that in regard to micturition. From his earliest days the child has been taught that the bladder can be evacuated at certain times and places only. When this has to be done in unusual places—such as in bed during illness or from a small boat—the greatest difficulty may be experienced in commencing the act. In the same way our thoughts have become fixed. Some persons are abnormally sensitive about clothes or daring to remonstrate against an obviously erroneous order and in our present polite days, of even contradicting a misstatement at a scientific meeting.

Much of modern education has been freed of mental submission engendered by the older education which demanded strict obedience and a large amount of unnatural silence amongst children, a restriction from which many never recovered. The child was to "be seen but not heard". Most of the younger readers of this page can have little conception of the restraints on the so-called "well brought up" children prior to 1910. Now, too often, we see the opposite extreme of young persons who have no respect for age, tradition or authority or indeed for anything which interferes with their own commonly selfish views. Since, however, submission to some degree is necessary in any community in the interest of others, it is certainly desirable that the restraint should be imposed at an age when it is least irksome and commonplace.

Religion of many kinds tends to promote submission, and most religions have their dogma the unquestioning belief and submission to which is essential, indeed, it is the refusal to accept such dogma which has caused so much controversy in the past. Christianity teaches that a man ought to be content with his lot and do his best to perform whatever humble tasks are allotted to him. A vast variety of reasons are given for this. The spirit is chastened in a multitude of ways. Eastern religions promote an excessive submission, a fatalism. What is unavoidable is the will of Allah is accepted without question, "Glory be to Allah". Throughout the East we see traces of a similar acceptance of circumstance. The Arabic word "malesh" carries that suggestion in its meaning.

The various types of rebellion are dealt with in regard to the Escapes and Continuation of Conflicts.

Resistance – A characteristic of submission is the resistance to change or to anything which disturbs the even tenor or peace of mind. It is so much more comfortable to drift on downstream than to fight against it. This occurs noticeably as might be expected in those whose occupations involve unusual submission to regulations. The civil servant, whether he be highly or lowly placed, is notoriously static in outlook. The policeman has his routine type of enquiry, the civil servant has his regulations, the politician has his party, the mediocre scientist and the doctor who "have made up their minds" tend to have over-dogmatic views. The older the individual the more fixed and resistant to change he tends to become. Many persons when they "make up their minds" really find it easiest to submit to having done so and stick to their opinions against all opposition as if in a debating society.

Mental Mechanisms Commonly Used in Submission

These mechanisms have been variously described. They may be described as defence mechanisms as they may be used as a defence against any form of mental disquiet. They may be considered mechanisms by which the frustrated instincts obtain satisfaction in an oblique way which is acceptable to the community, or in a more general biological way they may be looked upon as mechanisms by which the individual adapts himself to his environment.

Rationalisation – Those who have submitted often support their resistance and their action by arguments which are not based on reason but on emotion. This is known as rationalisation. We all know how ardently a politician will defend the tenets of the party to which he has submitted and put up quite untenable arguments. Such men are not necessarily intentional hypocrites when they preach one thing, e.g., equality, and do another. They humbug themselves even more than they irritate others by their inconsistencies. The use of the process of rationalisation is not, however, confined to submission. It sometimes provides a convenient excuse for a certain line of conduct which is to the benefit of the individual concerned, directly or indirectly. Thus, the petty thief, who may not be dishonest in many matters, may argue that he is as entitled to the article as the possessor. Or a man may be unconsciously jealous of the success of another although he hotly resents the idea being suggested. Even a scientific man may refuse to accept an essential modification of his discoveries, for "good reasons". Harvey, who discovered the circulation of the blood, refused to believe that there were lymphatics. Simpson, who first used chloroform, did not support the work of Lister, the man who made modern surgery possible, nor indeed did many of the distinguished surgeons of London, some of whom put forward reasoned statements why Lister should not be appointed to King's College. Professional jealousy and the fact that a prophet has no honour in his own country, is possibly dependent on a similar mentality which refuses to accept the existence of capability in an individual known in other spheres to be ordinary. It is in part too, a refusal to accede power to others who do not wear the same "school tie" or belong to the same herd.

In the process of submission it is possible to differentiate certain mental processes, but it will be recognised that they all have the same aim, the promotion of content and happiness and the avoidance of mental pain or conflict. In each it is evident that the agreeable mental state is attained by preventing the disagreeable thought reaching consciousness in a form that it can be recognised. There is some discussion as to how far these processes may be conscious or unconscious. As we said, the greatest contribution of Freud was that he postulated a dynamic unconscious mind which does such things in such a way that the instincts are satisfied yet the conscious self, which is so influenced by the opinion of the community, is appeased.

Repression

Repression of Disagreeable Thoughts – Emotional Forgetting

In relation to forgetting and errors it has been observed in many cases that commonly (but not always), things forgotten or mistakes made are related to disagreeable or undesired thoughts regarding those things.

This removal from consciousness of such disagreeable material appears to be a fundamental process which promotes the happiness and content of the individual and is known as *repression*. The process is therefore of the greatest importance in adapting the individual to his environment.

Freud considered that the disagreeable thoughts were repressed into the unconscious by the "censor" who is, so to speak, in charge of our happiness and mental well-being. There may be some disagreement amongst psychologists regarding the actual repressing force; indeed, Freud appears to have avoided discussing its nature in detail, but a conflict of words must not blind us to the undoubted existence of the process which is accepted by all schools of psychology.

The existence of the process has been clearly proved by the study of soldiers suffering from various forms of mental illness which were found to be based on the intensely disagreeable experiences of war. The experience is forgotten but in a singularly complete way. Sometimes indeed, in the case of soldiers, quite large periods of time appear to have been forgotten following the shock of the experience. The shock itself may be mental, physical or both. Loss of memory of the happenings immediately before an accident in civil life is relatively common and in hypnosis it is possible, by suggestion, to recall from memory a very large number of experiences, pleasant or painful. In the case of the war neuroses, as they are called, it has been found that the recall of the happenings concerned give rise to most expressive and painful emotions such as may have been produced at the original time of the experience – a phenomenon known as abreaction.

The repression is not, however, complete during sleep and the disagreeable thought may appear in "fear" or "desire dreams".

In some cases the processes do not depend on consciousness, but in others the disagreeable or "evil" thought has been "put out of the mind" by an effort of will, and it is recognised treatment to exhort those who suffer "not to think" of the disagreeable thing which troubles them. Indeed, this treatment is beneficial in a very wide variety of sorrows, from the loss of a lover to the tooth-ache. The average person represses all thought of death and seldom refers to it except as part of the inevitable or as a joke. In the latter he shows that there is an existing conflict with his security instincts.

Some psychologists differentiate between suppression and repression, one being conscious and the other not, but different psychologists use the terms in varying senses. Confusion is probably best avoided by using the term "suppression" as referring to conscious effort since Freud considered "repression" as an unconscious activity.

Repression of Instinctive Responses

A process of repression is seen also in relation to the instincts. We have seen that the various instincts demand satisfaction (because possibly the stimuli concerned are constantly arising), but it is evident that the rules of the community to which we belong do not allow of their unfettered indulgence and to these rules, for various reasons, we pay regard. It is, indeed, as if some variety of civilised response had been superimposed upon the instinctive response. We are not necessarily violent with the individual who shoves his way before us, nor are we necessarily rude to the person who is rude to us. Different communities of herds demand different responses. In certain groups there are certain things which are "not done". The instinct of the herd has commonly a repressing effect upon the instincts concerning nutrition, protection, sex and power. Thus, in war-time the instinct of the herd which demands emphasis to duty may completely repress the natural emotion of fear which is concerned with personal protection.

This variety of repression bears a considerable resemblance to the inhibition of reflexes and such response can undoubtedly be taught to animals. Thus, a dog may learn not to steal from the table, or to chase sheep, in other words, not to obey its natural instincts in a natural way. When two reflexes compete with one another for a final common path that which is most essential for the survival of the individual or his race takes precedence. Thus, the scratch movement of the hind leg of a dog which occurs if the saddle area is tickled, is inhibited if the animal is pinched.

It would seem that the community responses take precedence over the personal response if the individual is to survive happily within the community.

The Nature of Repression

The exact nature of process of repression is unknown, but Rivers has suggested that it is akin to the well-known inhibitory effect of the higher parts of the nervous system upon the lower, seen typically in the damping of the knee jerk by the pyramidal system.

It has been described as essentially an inability to face reality, a refusal of the personality to allow into consciousness any thought which is disagreeable, antisocial or which runs contrary to the communal or spiritual codes to which we adhere. By doing so it promotes the happiness of the individual and avoids him pain. This we have already noted is a function of the elementary nervous system in all animals. Repression may be considered simply as the mental analogue of the simple protective reflex of the spinal cord.

In relation to forgetting the immediate advantage of forgetting is self-evident as in the case of the simple spinal reflex. It is an immediate response which may subsequently be superseded by a higher response. This may make us eventually post the letter which we have earlier forgotten – really did not wish – to post just as we may control the reflex withdrawal of a finger from which a friend or doctor is attempting to extract a foreign body.

In regard to what has been described as the repression of the primary instincts by the social or spiritual instincts it is a little more difficult to see that the process is quite the same as that described. It is easier to consider the responses as of the nature of a conditioned response or inhibition superimposed upon the unconditioned response. Psychologists, however, with their characteristic desire to repress biological and physiological terms prefer to consider that the conscious educated system considers the normal response to the instinct harmful or antisocial and refuses to recognise it. The difference is one of words, the processes referred to are the same.

All are agreed that the instinctive response is altered, in the words of modern psychology it is modified by the censor, in the words of biology by a process of conditioning through the influence of the herd. It will however be realised that this process differs from the conditioned reflex in that it is the response which becomes "conditioned" and not the stimulus.

Sublimation – By this is meant the substitution for the normal response of the frustrated instinct by another response more acceptable to the community or to consciousness the censorship of which has been determined, by the spiritual and social codes accepted by the individual. One of the best examples is the sublimation of the sex instinct which we have seen, in relation to the herd instinct, is very materially controlled by the codes of the community. It is often seen that the childless woman exercises her maternal instincts by lavishing kindness on pets, and in taking an active part in the conduct of institutions especially those concerned with the care of the young. She may adopt a cause, especially one designed to assist those who, in her unconscious eyes, like children, need help. She is not indeed very different, mentally at least, from the hen who may rear ducklings, or the historic vixen who, by ancient legend suckled Romulus the founder of Rome, or the cow who submits to a milking machine. It is the instinct of the female to lavish protection and food on whoever wants it. Some generous-minded psychologists claim that a large proportion of prostitutes are actuated by such maternal rather than more material motives. Many believe that love is essentially sublimated sex, but the matter is much debated and is discussed in relation to "Love".

Sublimation of the instincts is evident in the popularity of all literature and drama bearing on feeding, fighting or sex, stories of which bulk so largely on the stage, cinema screen and in popular novels. Games too, probably play a similar part in stimulating a healthy rivalry between those concerned and thus sublimating the competitive characteristic of animal life.

The various processes which make submission with happiness possible have sometimes been presented in another way and this is well seen in the case of sublimation. It can be held, for example, that the instinct although submerged in the unconscious is still possessed of energy which must gain expression, and if it does not do so in the normal way will do so in another, like a spring which is obstructed and finds a more distant outlet.

Inversion – This is essentially the process underlying the fable of the fox and the grapes. The fox could not reach them, therefore concluded they were sour. The process is seen in many forms, thus a man cannot get a certain post, he therefore minimises the post. Business men, a little conscious of their own educational deficiencies, tend to consider academic persons as being devoid of business sanity. University men often impoverished, fondly imagine that business men have no mentality for anything except making money. A man leaving a post may believe that he resigned rather than that he was dismissed.

In the more practical professions such as engineering and architecture, we see the frequent jibing of the practical man who could not get through his examination, at the futility of examinations. In medicine, the man who has been unable to get through the matriculation examination and who takes a less qualification, commonly decries the value of a university degree, while later it is common to see a man who has not obtained a post in a certain university or firm to make disparaging remarks regarding it.

Projection is a somewhat similar phenomenon and is a common method of avoiding blame. It was seen in the early part of the war when German propaganda accused minorities of offences when in reality the Germans were guilty or about to be guilty of similar offences.

This is however a much more fundamental reaction than at first appears, and is seen in many forms. There is apparently an inherent tendency in human beings to shift the blame or responsibility for errors. In its earliest form it is seen when the small boy says that the other boy broke the window. The statement may or may not be true, but the making of it safeguards the security of the person saying it. Subsequently if a wrong decision at any meeting is made, someone is blamed, but in moments of greater national crisis a scapegoat has to be found and may be actually executed. To the onlooker it is merely "the pot calling the kettle black".

We commonly find that a man will accuse another of faults which he has himself or even the reverse – praise qualities in another which the third person sees in neither. This form of mutual back-scratching is notorious in those institutions in an attempt to demonstrate the "quality" of the institution to which they themselves belong.

A somewhat similar projection is common in conversations with animals. We put into words what we imagine they would like to say, but really what we would say if we were similarly placed.

Other well-known examples of projection are those of the bad student who dwells extensively upon the inefficiencies of his teachers and examiners, or of the lovelorn lady who imagines that all attractive men are in love with her and often chooses those with whom she comes in professional relationship as the object of her affections. Dentists, clergymen, chaffeurs and doctors who have opportunity of intimacy or even a solitary male in a railway carriage become the unfortunate objects of attention and may even be accused of attempted rape if they decline. Fortunately both medicine and law are familiar with such cases. The intense appeal of certain stage stars to some members of the opposite sex is also a form of projection, but sometimes the projection reaches the realm of phantasy. A widow may be visited by the ghost of her husband whom she will not believe to be dead, and many a maiden secures "a better man" in her dreams than would be possible in actual life. Symbolic, too, are bridal veil and ring of the nun who, as she takes her vow, becomes the bride of Christ and promises to devote her life to Him.

By the projection the individual obtains satisfaction of the wish to be attractive or to be considered free of guilt.

Why one person submits and another continues to resist is an interesting problem. Sometimes submission and resistance may alternate. It would seem that, generally, health and strength are important determining factors, and thus it is that we commonly see illness and mental depression together until the patient, if the illness is prolonged, has learnt to use the mental mechanisms which are so important in promoting mental peace and happiness.

9

CONTINUANCE OF CONFLICT

Submission is seldom complete, indeed, from time to time everyone rebels against things, in thoughts and words if not in deeds. The horse "kicks over the traces", the dog runs away, the child in whom restraint is not so complete may become petulant if not actually rebellious.

In the adult, however, severe conflict becomes a much more serious matter. We have already noted the effect of experimental conflict in animals. The animal which has been trained to react to an oblong and a circle gets into a state of great mental unrest when it has to decide the exact significance of an oval. In man similar causes are extremely common. The individual has to choose and cannot make the choice. The instincts or urges pull different ways.

Such continuance of conflict we see in the woman who cannot make up her mind to get married. She cannot balance the satisfactions to be gained and those which are to be lost. It may be that comparative comfort of the father's home has to be exchanged for the pleasure of being a "young man's slave", or a profession or work which brings in a handsome dress allowance has to be given up in exchange for penurious domesticity. There is often the problem of leaving aged and infirm parents, indeed, there are the many subjects which occupy the problem columns of the women's page of so many weekly journals.

For a man there are many similar problems. His getting married may interfere with his professional prospects. He may no longer have money to spare for foreign study. Different posts offer different opportunities.

All these, however, are insignificant compared with the great problem of wartime in which the instinct of self-preservation is in conflict with the instinct of the herd which demands that "England expects that every man this day will do his duty". The man may not even be afraid when faced with danger, but he is afraid of being afraid and of letting himself and his colleagues down. Often he succeeds in compensating and may be very successful until some minor injury or excessive fatigue undermines his strength, and his compensation fails and he is overcome by the threat to his security and becomes a victim of *anxiety neurosis*.

Physical fear is in a curious position. It is a perfectly normal reaction to a physical threat especially to those with imagination, but those who experience the emotion are commonly ashamed of it especially in the presence of others. They may compensate by remarkable and even foolhardy exhibitions of bravery, especially in war-time when such compensation is to be encouraged. In the last war it was found that an unusually large proportion of officers, invalided because of anxiety neurosis, had decorations for bravery (Schneider), and many a winner of the Victoria Cross has later frankly admitted that he was acutely afraid at the time of his heroic act.

Such conduct is the true bravery of devotion to duty, i.e. to the herd, and is exactly the reverse of that of the boasting braggart who is trying to hide the fact that he is really a coward in whom the instinct of self-preservation is uppermost. The subject has been discussed under Fear.

It may be that the anxiety is about work. The teacher may feel that he is no longer able to "get it across" or control his class, the research worker does not find that his observations work out as he had hoped, or that others will not believe his conclusions. He forgets temporarily that few investigations are straightforward according to plan and that many of the greatest discoveries have been disbelieved by quite eminent men. The anxiety may be financial, most people being quite forgetful that starvation is of very rare occurrence in a normal peace-time world.

Anxiety over examinations is very common, indeed a small proportion of undergraduates have to give up their studies because of it. If, however, they reach the stage of examination they put up quite good performances. This anxiety is not, however, to be confused with nervousness during the examination which is a condition which comes on acutely and is not present prior to the examination. The subject is pale and trembling. Too often, unfortunately this condition is associated with lack of preparation, but if not it rapidly passes off as the examination proceeds. In each there is frustration of the power urge and there may be a threat, real or imagined, to security.

The separation of anxiety neurosis from other neurotic states was made by Freud, in 1865, who considered it to be due to sexual stimulation without complete gratification, but although the term has been retained generally its original meaning has been lost except to Freud's most ardent disciples. Actually we all recognise minor degrees of anxiety in our friends, and our friends bring ours to our notice. Only the more acute states are brought to the notice of the physician.

It is generally accepted that there is a considerable "hereditary" factor in anxiety. Anxious children like those with phobias, are the offspring of anxious, worrying parents, but whether the anxiety is bred in the nervous system or depends on the post-natal association between parent and child is not certain. In such persons the immediate cause of the anxiety is almost any problem which normally confronts the average man.

Anxiety, like fear, cannot be considered abnormal. Every normal person feels anxious about different things from time to time. It is only when the anxiety becomes irrational that it becomes abnormal. Often the anxiety can be allayed by a good talk with someone who understands. Many psychologists hold that, in many instances, the basic cause of the anxiety is not the immediate conscious worry or conflict but some circumstance in early life which has given a deeper significance to the conflict. Thus, a child of an anxious parent who has always been warned to take care, to be a success in life, etc., etc. is liable to be self-centred or have what Freud called an inflated ego libido and have the instinct of self-preservation unduly developed and find it more than usually difficult to respond to the call of the herd to risk his life in war. How different it is from the state of the child who has been taught that it is his duty and privilege to fight for his country if it needs him. The anxiety may not, however, be personal, but may depend on the possible danger to a loved one.

The symptoms produced are essentially those of "restlessness" in the nervous system and exhaustion. Most of us have experienced this at some period in the war. There is difficulty in going to sleep and troublesome dreams – in war-time battle dreams, in peace-time the various events of the day. There is difficulty in concentration, general weariness, lack of interest and tenseness, a tendency to be unduly alarmed, e.g., at anything which sounds like an air-raid siren. There may be disorders of judgment and irritability and a tendency to excessive alcohol, tobacco and petty rebellion against convention or authority.

In the severe cases, seen amongst soldiers in war-time, a functional stuporous state like unconsciousness is described, associated with acute terror, with dilated pupils, cold sweat, trembling and inability to perform any movement. Breathing may be shallow. Subsequently there may be mental confusion and loss of memory.

We all recognise the worriers of the world. They are obviously upset by a quite minor illness, when there is anything essential to do they fuss unduly, they insist in being much too early for their train, they are in trouble about their luggage and a hundred other little things which arise on a journey.

The chronic effects of fear and anxiety, commonly known as worry, are well known. A man may "worry his guts out" which is a vulgar way of saying that his whole alimentary canal may become upset. Actually we know that worry is a most potent cause of dyspepsia and ulcer. It is well recognised too, that anxiety is an important factor in circulatory disease, notably high blood pressure, and it is believed that there may be reduced resistance of the body generally to illness. There can be little doubt that many illnesses tend to accentuate anxiety. Some of course do so because of the loss, financial and otherwise, sustained by the illness, but in some, notably influenza which depresses the nervous system generally, the misery produced may be so acute that suicide may result, or a prolonged period of depression may ensue.

The anxiety neurotic is to be differentiated from the patient suffering from conversion hysteria (see above) who has escaped from his conflict and is therefore in a state of mental rest. The hysteric recognises his symptoms as abnormal, and discusses them freely but cannot control them. For similar reasons a severely wounded man is seldom neurotic. He needs no escape, nor does the prisoner of war. It is of interest that American statistics indicate that conversion hysteria occurred almost entirely in N.C.O.'s and men, while so-called neurasthenia (i.e. anxiety neurosis) was most marked amongst officers, no doubt because of their additional responsibility.

(The term neurasthenia is now confined to nervous exhaustion with fatigue.)

In the nature of things an anxiety neurosis is a much more serious state than a conversion hysteria because of the exhaustion, and because there is often underlying the immediate conflict, conflicts of a more basal nature which have become fixed. A case may, however, commence as an anxiety neurosis but subsequently becomes one of hysteria, in which there is mental quietude. The chief difference between hysteria and anxiety is the mental state.

Treatment consists essentially of securing a relationship between the onset of the anxiety and the emotional cause of the conflict, but severe cases can only be dealt with by those who have had extensive experience of such cases.

Open conflict may take the robust form of open rebellion against the force which frustrates. The conflict may be personal or it may be on behalf of the herd. Those who rebel on behalf of the herd are those who support causes. They are the fighters of the world and are never defeatists. Theirs must be a world in which they must all be powerful. As a last resort they rely on their own physical power, often forgetful that in a modern world man cannot prevail against organisation, steel and modern explosives.

More often the rebellion of the adult is simply against that which restrains on behalf of the community. It is essentially a continuation of the rebellion against the authority of the parent or schoolmaster who failed to exercise authority properly, commonly because they have not been reasonable, have given excessive punishment or have been themselves unworthy. In a democracy there is a traditional conflict against the state on behalf of the freedom of the individual or the various herds of which the community is composed. There is, however, a great variation of response amongst individuals. Some merely grumble volubly and are often guilty of the things they complain of, notably the laziness and inefficiency of others. Some pugnacious personalities appear to rebel almost on principle, they are the "difficult", uncompromising and contentious people of the world, so afraid of being thought inferior if they give way, that they fail completely to understand the feeling of others who may be involved. In their enthusiasm they bring more unhappiness into the world over which they have authority than they dream of. Often, however, they are the individuals who get things done because by ignoring the feelings of others they disturb the existing order of things which too often have become static and not infrequently full of the vested interest of those who run the particular show concerned. These vested interests are the dangers of a democracy for they are by no means confined to any special class of the community.

Summary of the Responses to Conflict

It is convenient to present the various types of response in the first instance in concise form in order to show the general picture in which it will be seen that in each type of response there are several degrees. Each normal person has his conflict and reacts to it in a normal way. The more emotional, excitable and unstable person gives an exaggerated response which, according to the degree of unstability, may merge into the irrational or pathological. It is, however, important to emphasise that there is no hard and fast line between the normal and what is deemed the abnormal, but that there is a graduation from one into the other. As has been said elsewhere "every man has a sane spot somewhere" and "all men are mad".

Submission

Normal. – Clothes, operations, loyalty.
Exaggerated – Feelings of inferiority, guilt, unworthiness, temporary depression, sycophancy.
Pathological – Delusions of persecution, prolonged depression, melancholia.

Escape

Normal – Jokes, phantasy (theatre, cinema), alcohol, hobbies, etc.
Exaggerated – The above to excess, fainting.
Pathological – Chronic alcoholism, hysteria and other illness, suicide.

Conflict and Frustration

Normal – Struggle against adversity, submission with compromise.
Exaggerated – Compensated inferiority giving conceit, old maidishness, rebellion, refusal of desirable operation, bossiness, bullying.
Pathological – Anxiety neurosis, mania, homicide, suicide.

From the above it will become apparent that the author does not differentiate between the psychoneuroses and incurable mental disease which is studied by psychiatrists, because it is held that any differentiation, although convenient from the point of view of prognosis, is psychologically artificial.

The Conceptions of Freud in Relation to a Biological Psychology

In view of the fact that in Britain it may be fairly said that psychotherapy is practised largely by those who adhere to the theories of Freud, a short statement of these theories may not be out of place, the more so as the development of the subject owes more to him than any other single individual. Many of the terms, which forever will be used in the subject, were first used by him, and through his genius we were provided, for the first time, with a dynamic view of mental activity.

In the first instance, it should be understood that the mental processes concerned must obviously be identical whatever terminology is used, and that the differences between the various schools of psychology are essentially different presentations and interpretations of the same facts.

Freud has succeeded in presenting the facts in a way which is at once as picturesque as it is dynamic. He gave his conceptions active personality. The total self which is presented to the world is the conscious Ego which is adapted to the environment through the Ego instincts. It corresponds largely to what has been described as the herd instinct. It keeps in check and censors the activity of the primary instincts which were classified as one—the Libido or Id—of which the all-important considered was the sexual instinct. Later he used the term Eros. In keeping the Libido in check the Ego has the assistance of the Super-ego which is analogous to the conscience which, according to our view; may be considered partly due to the herd instinct or more largely spiritual. A balance is maintained between the Ego and the Libido. Just as the Ego is considered to be the conscious self, the Libido is looked upon as being active in a deeper personality, the unconscious self. The Libido is a wild animal thing always demanding gratification. It seeks pleasure and avoids pain. If it cannot be satisfied in the conscious reality of a modern world it becomes repressed into the unconscious mind which is considered to be another psychic system. Here they are not simply latent as they were in earlier views of the unconscious, notably that of Samuel Butler, but they have a definite dynamic character and still strive to obtain gratification in some other way. What have been described as escapes, substitutions and sublimations become wish-fulfilments and evidence of the internal struggle.

In sleep, the conscious Ego and Super-ego are in abeyance with the result that the desires and fears of the Libido obtain full gratification in the dream, while occasionally similar wishes and fears become evident in forgetting and other errors. It is in relation to these indeed, that Freud made his first and most generally agreed contribution, although it is obviously not correct to consider all dreams to be of this kind.

Many of the earlier writers on psychology have discussed the subject of instinct in almost exactly the same terms as moderns do the "unconscious" of Freud. The independence of instinct is possibly most evident in the writings of Bergson who saw it antagonised by conscious intellect. General reading of this kind indeed indicates the evolution of the idea of the "unconscious mind"– which may be described as the instinctive mind – but it is just a little doubtful if it is really as unconscious as Freud and his supporters would have us believe.

This fundamental idea of the personality of Id is not so new as at first sight appears to those who have not troubled to search beyond Freud's teachings, although admittedly by applying the conception to a modern life he imbued that occult personality with a new and modernised vitality. The Id bears a most remarkable resemblance to the Ka or soul of the ancient Egyptians. In the Hedonism of the ancient Greeks we have a similar philosophy of life based on the simple avoidance of pain and pursuit of pleasure. Such a philosophy, especially the avoidance of pain, itself is based on the natural behaviour of all animals. It is this fundamental and incontrovertible basis in biology which unwittingly is the stable element in Freud's theories without which the universe he has created would fall to pieces. To those who study the nervous system it is evident that the elementary reactions of the nervous system, which are quite independent of the brain, are those which protect the body against pain, and even in the lowest form of animal life with little or no nervous system, we find this protective withdrawal from injury exercised by single cells capable of contraction. Thus, we begin to realise that the avoidance of injury or its counterpart, pain, is the fundamental consideration of the nervous system and of the mind alike in almost every psychological school of thought.

Other ancient views suggest the occurrence of an entity with the dynamic quality of a personality but other than that which is normal. Thus, the insane were considered to be possessed of devils – and various allusions to such conceptions occur in ordinary parlance.

All the Freudian theory given above is roughly accepted although it need not be expressed in the same terms. Freud's theories regarding so-called infantile sexuality have not, however, received the same general acceptance, nor has his view that neuroses are always due to some disturbance with the sex life of the individual, for even allowing for the fact that he used the term sex as applying to the primary instincts upon which life depends, there can be little doubt that he considered chiefly sex in its usual sense to be the dominant urge.

The psychoanalytic method which is essentially an analysis of the associations and which we owe primarily to Freud, when used by Freud's adherents, invariably uncovers a sexual basis of the abnormal state under consideration, but in the hands of others, other and just as potent causes are revealed.

The great and most justifiable criticism and Freud's view is that which is so often true of any new view, even if when it amounts to a great discovery, is that it tries to explain too much and lacks general perspective. It may be true that his views are specially applicable to mental illness and diseased minds, but for the average intelligent student of the subject as a whole, the views lack perspective and fail to give adequate consideration of the normal average mind. Adler has pointed out the Freud paid too little importance to the power urge although he did not use the term. Trotter has emphasised that he laid too little stress on the repressing factor which is commonly herd instinct, while to others, like McDougall, Freud failed to give any motive purposes to human life much higher than that of the animals. This may, alas, seem true of many humans, for there is little doubt that the minds of men and of nations have not evolved to the same extent as their bodies. Life would indeed be a colourless mirage if that were all – a tale –

> Told by an idiot full of sound and fury
> Signifying nothing.

Fortunately there are many amongst us who feel otherwise.

10

PERSONALITY

Personality is one of those things which it is easier to appreciate than define. It is the whole human being considered in relation to the society in which he lives. It is somewhat different from the individuality which exists independently of the social situation.

Personality appears to depend on a number of qualities, physical, intellectual, emotional, social, moral and spiritual. It is the sum of the reactions to the master motives of the average person with whom there is inevitable comparison.

The physical qualities are shown by his health and energy, his appearance, expression and habits.

The intellectual qualities are shown by his capability in a vast number of directions.

The emotional qualities are shown by his spirit, cheerfulness, enthusiasm, industry and thrust.

Social qualities include all the things the average man likes in social life. Kindness, co-operation, adaptability, tolerance etc., etc.

Moral qualities include reliability, honesty, thoroughness.

Spiritual qualities include the material acts, idealism, love, sympathy, forgiveness, respect for God, interest in the future and welfare of mankind.

A consideration of what has already been said indicates that it is the resultant of the total forces concerned with the formation of the mind, the heredity together with the personal experience of the individual as shown by his relations towards his fellows and their institutions.

It is possible to classify personalities in a vast variety of ways. The classification of Sadler is as follows:

The Deficients who depend on others and are mostly in an asylum. The Criminal or delinquent. The Depraved or perverted. The Stupid or backward. The Isolated or lonely. The Emotional or cheerful. The Neurotic or frustrated. The Eccentric or queer. The Moody or depressed. The Insane or demented. The Diseased. The Well-balanced.

They have also been divided by Jung into three main groups: The extroverts who are the cheerful optimists with a good herd instinct, the introverts who are thoughtful and lonely, good and scholarly, imaginative, sensitive, and the ambiverts who are partly both.

It would seem that personality depends largely on hereditary factors, for in any family is commonly found an individual who, as we say "takes after" the parents or grandparents. It is quite reasonable to believe that just as their external appearances resembles that of their parents, the minute arrangement of their neurones do also and so influence their reactions and capabilities. In an ideally ordered eugenic society we might breed out its undesirable features just as the fighting propensities have been largely bred out of the bull-terrier, or the kicking out of carriage horses. So far such breeding has been confined to the few who think, but it will be realised that many parents do what they can to prevent the marriage of their families with undesirable traits of health or mind. But although nature deals the cards, the individual plays his own game of life, and a great deal can be done to assist him to do so properly, to combat antisocial or undesirable tendencies if they are recognised early.

Personality then may be looked upon as the outward expression of the multitudes of patterns of mental activity which have been partly inherited and partly acquired.

We may compare the personality to a musical instrument. We may play on it many tunes in many or a limited number of keys, but the essential quality of the particular instrument remains. Moods are seen in the type of piece we play, sacred, martial, dance and so on.

Personality would appear to depend, like other unconscious, mental activities, on a large number of definite patterns of thought. The exact group of patterns in operation at any given time may cause considerable change of mood. Some personalities change their moods much more frequently than others, especially women. We sometimes say that we met a certain person who was in this or that kind of mood. The mood is sometimes determined by circumstances, the individual may be depressed because of the overwhelming effects of some misfortune, or elated because of some success, but it is the sum total of the moods which makes up the personality.

Personality is as a rule fairly stable and does not change, at least suddenly, over a period of years. Changes in personality are, however, often seen as a result of environment, emotional stress, and even hormonal changes. Thus, a prolonged sojourn in prison, such as may occur in war-time, or a severe illness may be effective in this way. We commonly say that a person has never been the same since the death of a loved one, or a professional or business disappointment. In women distinct changes in personality are apparent as a result of tumours of the adrenal cortex which produce a state of virilism in which feminine characteristics are lost and male-like personality appears. In some women the menstrual periods make such profound changes of moods as would be indistinguishable from a change of personality if they were prolonged.

In disease there has been observed commonly since the earliest times, certain personalities associated with pathological or subnormal states. The cheerfulness of the tuberculous contrasts vividly with the misery of the dyspeptic.

When the sum of the mental reactions change we say that the personality changes. In different plays an actor may be called upon to play the parts of characters with very different personalities, but many instances are on record where, for emotional reasons, the personality has actually changed for prolonged periods or has become dissociated into two or more parts.

Probably the best known is Stevenson's story of Dr. Jekyll and Mr. Hyde. By day Dr. Jekyll was a respected member of society, by night a footpad, more animal than human. Such cases exist in real life but their story is not told so well. Another well-known case, quoted by James, is that of the Rev. Ansel Bourne who one day drew money from the bank and was seen to enter a tramcar. This was the last he remembered. Two months later he awoke in a fright and asked those in the house how he came to be where he was. He had rented a shop, stocked it with stationery and confectionery and had carried on quite a successful business under the name of A.J. Bourne. When he awoke he had no remembrance of his shopkeeping activities. From time to time we read of such cases in the newspapers.

Morton Prince put on record the remarkable case of Miss Beauchamp whose personality completely changed for long periods several times. (1) She was an impressionable who had an unhappy home life. At 16 she ran away, at 18 she became a nurse and had an affair with a man which gave her severe emotional shock. (2) Her whole personality changed to state B_1 during which she was a student and which lasted six years. This was a reality state but she was hampered by ill health. She was rather shy, weakly, studious, sociable. One day in the presence of Dr. Prince she was changed after another emotional shock. B_1 became latent and B_4 appeared. In this personality she was assertive, bad-tempered, quarrelsome, vain, disliking everybody. (3) During a fourth period, personalities B_1 and B_4 alternated and had no knowledge of each other.

A fifth period began during deep hypnosis when a personality B_2 appeared which seemed to be a fusion of B_1 and B_4 with the good and bad qualities of each.

B_3 was a personality which was found to occur during the time she was B_1. She was an impish child who called herself Sally and did what she liked, but Sally B_3 was aware of B_2 and could control B_1 but was obliterated by B_4 which did not recognise B_3.

These cases are somewhat gross, but it will be realised that similar instances of persons leading a very marked double life occur. A church elder has been known to run a flat for his girl friend. Or he may have Sunday and week-day codes of ethics. On the Sunday he is full of ideals and good thoughts, and on Monday would do all he can to get the better of his neighbour, consoling himself that business is business. Or again we have certain codes of fairness which are emotionally cold but when roused we say that all is fair in love and war.

It would seem that a theme can dominate all the thoughts for the time such as occurs in the case of the great actor or barrister. Moreover in such cases the theme has a strong emotional background. If you can only wake up the British lion, it will fight. Sometimes a hobby or vice dominate all thoughts. We all know people who take up activities or causes and run them to death and then drop them.

The actual personality which we display from time to time is always coloured by emotion. That in turn may be affected by health especially early health when personality is in process of formation.

It is often said that doctors are callous, and tend to consider their patients as cases. That is true, but up to a point it is a great advantage as patients can be treated or advised without emotion. This is true of professional advice of any kind whether it be that of an architect or a stockbroker. He may, however, have his advice coloured by his emotions and experience. That is why doctors do not treat their own families as a rule. It should be emphasised that the really good doctor does not ignore entirely the personality of his patient, indeed, he takes full cognisance of it and includes it in the case. Some cases need more sympathy and tact than others. Some men can be talked to as man to man, others become babies when they are ill, or imagine they are ill.

Personality is important in psychology from many points of view, indeed, many would make it the essence of psychology for, more than anything else, it represents the unity of the organism we know as a human being. To the academic psychologists with a philosophical background, the personality is the outward expression of an immaterial entity the mind. To the Freudians it is the resultant of the conscious and the unconscious minds reacting together in relation to human society.

From the point of view of medical psychology it is important as it may indicate the basal complexes which may underlie the abnormal state which is requiring treatment.

While personality is quite a distinct entity there is little doubt that environment may alter it slowly but quite appreciably. Thus, a man may cease to be so aggressive or truculent, and so on.

It is such changes, whether environmental or hormonal, which make it difficult to accept "Gestalt psychology", in which mental reactions are considered to be dependent on a fixed inherent and hereditary pattern which reacts as a whole and cannot be broken up into stimulus or response. The pattern is considered to have an insight or purpose. This psychological conception is possibly of value in so far as it emphasises wholeness of response and its evolution, but it appears to give to the individuality a fixity of mentality which is certainly more evident in Germany, where pattern psychology has been developed, than in most other countries. Admittedly, the gross failure in war-time of distinguished civilians to adapt themselves to changed conditions does suggest that pattern psychology may be more important than many of us imagined.

11

DREAMS AND HUMAN BEHAVIOUR

Dreams have a special interest to all psychologists as they indicate an activity of the brain which is outwith the domain of ordinary consciousness. The dream may be defined as an awareness of streams of impulses which do not reach that consciousness which is in relation to the external environment.

The psychoanalytic view of dreams is that they represent essentially the wishes and fears of the unconscious which in the ordinary way are not allowed to enter consciousness. The dreams are essentially wish-fulfilment. The behaviourist would believe that dreams are the result of stimuli which arise at the periphery. The two views are not, however, so incompatible as at first appears. It is convenient in the first instance, as in the case of forgetting, to consider that there are what might be described as memory dreams and those which might be described as emotional dreams, while there are dreams in which the two types may overlap

Memory Dreams

These dreams are a simple continuation of the activity of the day. After a voyage or a long day's motoring our dreams may be those involving the sensation of motoring for sailing. These may be repeated on several nights immediately following. Or the dream may consist of an experience obviously dictated by a story in a book we have been reading shortly before going to sleep. Often the details of various items get mixed up although their origin remains recognisable. On a purely physiological basis it is easy to believe that certain ideas, or experiences, have set certain chains of neurones in action and that the impulses, being self-propagating, have not subsided by the time sleep occurs. After a lapse of years the author recommenced to play badminton and that night dreamt most vividly of the last occasion when he played badminton in a hut in the Sinai Desert. In such circumstances, it is easy to imagine that the peripheral impulses set up impulses along pathways which had years before been in use together. In general it can be said that dreams are commonly of subjects of recent occurrence in the life of the dreamer.

An interesting series of dreams were described by a physiologist in a German prisoners of war camp in 1917. When at first food was scarce conversation and dreams were commonly about food. Sex was conspicuously absent. When, however, parcels from England began to arrive and the security instincts were reasonable, sex stories and sex dreams became a feature of life.

The effect of air-raid sirens has been very interesting and has demonstrated the "memory" factor in determining the content of a dream produced by the same stimulus in different persons.

In one it caused a dream of bees in flight, in another it was first interpreted as a warning against skating on dangerous ice preceded by a dream of curling in which the sound of a curling stone on ice awakened a train of "unconscious memories". In another it caused a sensation of hunger, it would seem because, for many years the dreamer dined in a room in which the sound of trams and of cars changing gear was usual. The significance of such dreams is commonly recognised by those who make no pretentions to psychological knowledge. Somewhat similar dreams are apparently seen from time to time in pet animals which may be observed to exhibit many of the signs of the chase, such as barking or the making of running movements.

Emotional Dreams

The emotional dream is also quite a distinct entity. It has a similar nature to the day-dream. Freud has pointed out that dreams represent the primitive wishes and fears of the unconscious mind uncensored by social or spiritual restraints of consciousness. Thus to dream of death is to wish harm or fear the death of the individual concerned. The dream of a child that he has unlimited choice in a fruit or sweet shop is an obvious wish dream.

It is in this field that the work of Freud has its most universal acceptance, but it is unfortunate that he apparently refused to recognise the existence of the simpler memory dreams and that he gave a sexual interpretation to so many of the symbols of which the dreams are composed. Undoubtedly, too, he exaggerated the importance of infantile life and neglected recent events.

There can be little doubt that most normal individuals have from time to time wishes and fears which they have never voiced, wishes and fears of which they may be ashamed as they conflict too fiercely with the social and ethical codes to which they subscribe. Such thoughts flit through the mind during moments of solitary leisure but are not usually allowed into consciousness. They concern those we love and those we hate, thoughts of ambition and thoughts of failure.

Battle dreams are largely of this nature. The man may live again through the terrors and tortures of the battlefield with all its emotions and horrors and the conflicting emotions of the sense of duty and of self-preservation, many so horrible that he dare not think of them during consciousness. They are indeed forgotten in the interest of the happiness of the individual. He prefers not to think of them. When they are brought to consciousness of the patient by the psychoanalyst they usually give rise to severe emotional outbursts.

It has become recognised that in neurotic subjects the dreams which are commonly repeated are those which have a strong emotional basis and in patients such dreams may give a clue to the cause of the symptoms from which a patient may be suffering. Many psychologists now believe, however, that often the content of a dream is like day dreaming, so fortuitous that unless it is an oft-repeated dream any attempt at analysis may be misleading.

The Mixed Dream

Here we have a simple mixture of the memory and the emotional dream. The dream may have the setting of a recent experience. We find ourselves sailing or motoring with someone in regard to whom there is some emotional bias, or someone we hate becomes the villain in the story we have just been reading.

Dream Symbolism

As we have said, many dreams are readily recognised and analysable, but many are not so simple, and we owe it to Freud that it has become recognised that a dream may have a "latent content" different from what appears in the manifest dream. The object dreamt of may have only some of the qualities of the object it represents. Thus, as in a case, two red-hot pokers may represent spurting blood (Ross). What is dreamt of may be considered a symbol of something much more significant in the life of the individual.

Freudians would have us believe that the majority of the symbols dreamt of have a sexual significance. Thus, a pistol or a round hollow object with a hole in the end is a penis, when it may as readily be a gun. At the same time it will be admitted there is a great similarity in symbolism and those accustomed to the analysis of dreams become very adroit in appreciating the full significance of the symbols which are determined by the "latent content" of the dream.

By studying the closest association of the individual around the qualities of the object dreamt of it is often possible to obtain an insight into the significance of the symbol for the individual, while the distortions of the object may similarly be shown to have a significance. According to Freud the distortion is the result of the censorship. The dream has been aptly compared to the cartoon, and this is especially true of the composite cartoon in which two individuals may be shown as one, or the picture with a theme as we might see a public man portrayed as Jack the Giant-killer. The significance of the cartoon may not, however, be understood if we do not know the circumstances to which it refers. Thus, the idea to be conveyed regarding a cabinet minister may depend on the political colour of the paper on which it appears.

Sometimes the dream shows what is known as a "regression" to an earlier experience. Thus, a patient may, after a period of stress, dream of being frightened by an animal which in fact frightened him years before. Rivers quotes an instance of a patient who after an aeroplane accident dreamt of a Chinaman who had appeared in similar circumstances in childhood. The original appearance of the Chinaman was, however, not accounted for.

The Biological Function of the Dream

There has been considerable discussion as to whether the dream may not have some biological significance. Freud, as we have seen, considered the dream to be essentially a wish-fulfilment. Rivers, however, considered that dreams are attempts to solve during sleep conflicts which are disturbing to the waking life. He also suggests that at least some of the dream prepares the animal for activity appropriate to the stimulus. This is suggested by the study of sleeping animals, e.g. dogs, which commonly react with aggressive movements such as growling or barking, and it has been found that the sleeper might react differently to different kinds of stimuli.

Several psychologists have suggested that the dreams protect sleep in that in spite of the stimuli or conflict the subject does not awake. This, however, can only be partly true for the typical nightmare which is associated with intense sympathetic activity, indicated by the rapid heart, cold sweat and pallor, is incompatible with sleep and causes the subject to awake. This is what would be expected if we assume the current view that sleep is normally associated with, if not actually the result of, diminished sympathetic activity.

In the present state of our knowledge it is probably best to look upon the dream as akin to consciousness and free association, the content of the dream being largely haphazard and depending on a vast number of associations.

12

ILLUSION IN THE PSYCHOTHERAPEUTIC ENTERPRISE

Self-knowledge is possible only when the identification of subject and object takes place; that is, when scientific studies come to an end, and lay down all their gadgets of experimentation, and confess that they cannot continue their researches any further unless they can transcend themselves by performing a miraculous leap over into a realm of absolute subjectivity.

Introduction

To the Western mind the concept of *anatta* or 'no-Self' is initially both puzzling and threatening; puzzling because it is hard for the Self to consider its existence as being anything other than that which involves a distinction between Self and Other, and threatening because it consequently seems to undermine our very existence and understanding of the world. Western thought is built upon the notion of an individual Self/Soul/Ego, that is separate from, but interacts with, the world and other selves; Man's separation is depicted in the Book of Genesis, where the developing egocentricity of Adam and Eve leads to separation from God and expulsion from Eden; and much of Western philosophy can be seen to descend from Plato (with his preoccupation with the existence of souls) and Descartes (with his philosophy predicated on 'Cogito ergo sum').

Today, Western psychology is largely predicated on evolutionary theory and humans are no longer seen to be at the centre of the universe. Yet acceptance of the continuity of species and of our relative position in the universe has done little to affect our egocentricity, with our concern for self-image and self-esteem. Psychoanalytic thinking has contributed to the notion of a separate Self through Freud's tripartite conceptual apparatus, where the conscious ego strives to obtain a balance between the demands of external reality, the libidinal forces of the id and the restraining forces of the super-ego, the latter two both operating to some degree at an unconscious level. Thus, there is an implicit dichotomy between this 'psychodynamic' balance and external reality.

One reaction against psychodynamic thinking was the development in the 1960s of learning theory and behaviour therapy, where the idea of Self was absorbed into the over-inclusive term 'organism', and the Self-Other dichotomy continued under the guise of organism-stimuli. However, both the psychoanalytic and behavioural camps have led to various off-shoots, the former having spawned client centred therapy, gestalt therapy, group analysis, as well as various refinements of psychoanalytic theory, including theories that address the concept of Self centrally, while the latter has itself developed in sophistication and given rise to more cognitively based therapies. (Of course not all the developments and off-shoots now fit neatly into one camp or the other, and some schools of thought may have only tenuous links with either.)

So there is now a vast variety of therapeutic approaches available to the psychotherapist, yet in nearly all there is an implicit acceptance of the reality, in whatever disguished form, of a Self, separate from but interacting with other selves. It is this notion that this chapter wishes to address; it is not our intention to review the burgeoning literature on the Self, nor to provide a critical analysis of different theoretical approaches. Rather we shall attempt to suggest that the Buddhist concept *anatta* can enrich apparently diverse theoretical frameworks while acting as a point of contact between them. It will be argued that belief in the reality of a separate Self, rather than enhancing psychological well-being, actually leads to suffering. It follows that therapies that themselves accept uncritically the notion of Self are clinging to the suffering they aim to alleviate.

Anatta – The Buddhist Doctrine of 'No-Self'

The preceding section used the terms Self/Soul/Ego somewhat interchangeably, to refer to that human 'duality' which is separate and distinct from other aspects of the world. *Anatta* is the Buddhist doctrine of 'No-Self' or 'No-Soul'. It is not to be regarded as referring to that which is not Self, but rather to a *disconfirmation* of Self. We cannot seriously deny that we think and are aware, and use of terms such as 'we' and 'I' point to a distinction. But in Buddhism this distinction is illusory, a delusion that we cling to and which, like all attachments, gives rise to suffering. The practice of Zen Buddhism has as one of its aims the dismantling of this construct of a separate Self and all the constraints that go with it.

> When we practice zazen our mind always follows our breathing. When we inhale, the air comes into the inner world. When we exhale, the air goes out to the outer world. The inner world is limitless, and the outer world is also limitless. We say 'inner world' or 'outer world', but actually there is just one whole world. In this limitless world, our throat is like a swinging door. The air comes in and goes out like someone passing through a swinging door. If you think, 'I breathe,' the 'I' is extra. There is no you to say 'I'. What we call 'I' is just a swinging door which moves when we inhale and when we exhale. It just moves; that is all. When your mind is pure and calm enough to follow this movement, there is nothing: no 'I,' no world, no mind nor body; just a swinging door.

It is this 'limitlessness' that begins to emerge as the constraints of 'Self' are relinquished. (In Zen Buddhist meditation halls there often can be found a statue of 'Monju on the Beast'-Monju is the personification of our earnest and vigilant training in Buddhism, who sits on the 'Beast of Self' who never sleeps and whose eyes are always open!)

Self in Relation to Psychotherapy

Psychoanalysis

There has been much discussion as to whether 'ego', 'superego,' and 'id' are to be taken as a convenient conceptual scheme, as a structure that has a neurological referential basis, or as terms that translate readily into behavioural terminology. 'Ego' is itself used in various ways, though in general it describes a persons's ability to cope with the demands of day-to-day reality in the light of past experiences. Clients who are deemed able to withstand the rigours of psychoanalysis or psychoanalytical psychotherapy without, for example, undergoing a psychotic disintegration, are described as having sufficient 'ego-strength' for psychotherapy. The 'healthier' one's ego, the more one is able to cope with the demands of daily life.

According to contemporary psychoanalytic theory, an individual's 'sense of Self' goes through various developmental stages: from early identification with mother to gradual separation and the developing awareness of one's own boundaries. It generally is held that the nature of one's experiences during the early stages of separation will affect subsequent development of self-image and 'ego-functioning'. Some of these experiences may contribute to later 'pathological' behaviour that serves to maintain a 'strong' sense of Self. Hence 'strength' of self-concept does not readily correspond with psychological well-being. Psychoanalysis specifically aims to bring about more adaptive ego functioning by working through unconscious conflict. Changes in the nature of 'ego-defences' during therapy lead to greater accessibility of unconscious material. Thus, the unconscious is made conscious. Parallel to this development in ego function is a re-organised 'sense of Self'. But despite the often long and intensive nature of psychoanalytically based therapies, the goal does not reach beyond that of healthy/adaptive ego functioning and it is generally accepted that there will remain a sizeable residue of unconscious material.

However, this restrictive view has been challenged by a small number of psychoanalysts, most notably Jung and Fromm. Fromm in particular has attempted to relate psychoanalysis to Zen Buddhism, seeing the former as attempting to uncover a limited aspect of unconscious functioning, whereas the latter strives for the 'total experience' of the unconscious. He sees the ability to achieve this as being due in part to the regular practice of meditation. Meditation stimulates 'primary process' thinking thereby allowing direct experience of unconscious material:

> Where analysis aims to illuminate the unconscious with the clear light of reason, . . . Zen strives to eliminate the intellect, as a noxious interference, from the otherwise free flow of the unconscious. Analysis heightens awareness of self; Zen ideally eliminates self-awareness.

Various authors have advocated the use of meditation as an integral part of psychodynamic therapy. Kutz, for example, sees meditation as a 'cognitive therapeutic technique' whereby one sits as a detached observer of a process where thoughts and images enter the mind and disappear, feelings and sensations come and go, in a constant flow.

> Eventually, the meditator not only becomes aware of the content of thoughts and images, but also begins to recognise patterns and habits that dictate thought formation and dissolution.

Like Fromm, Kutz sees this 'cognitive' technique as leading to a shift towards more predominant primary process thinking, a mode of thinking that is largely 'intuitive', unbound by logical and formal rules, and essential for the cohesive integration of a sense of Self.

Unfortunately, Kutz does not pursue meditation or Buddhist practice beyond the stage of inducing a 'sense of Self' that is 'ineffable and experienced as feelings of inner trust and serenity'. He sees meditation rather as a 'primer' for psychotherapy. Kutz is rightly critical of the limited aims of conventional psychoanalytic thinking, but he himself stops short of S. Suzuki's 'limitlessness' by clinging to a notion of a Self: one that is an 'observer' during the process of meditation.

Cognitive Therapy

Over recent years there has been increasing attention paid towards therapies that focus specifically on the way our thinking affects emotion and behaviour, therapies that primarily have developed from the theories of Beck, Ellis and Kelly. However, Ponce traces the origins of the view that psychological suffering is a result of our 'construction' of reality, to the ancient Greek civilisation in the West, and the historical Buddha in the East; in support of the latter assertion he quotes from the opening passage of the *Dhammapada:*

> We are what we think.
> All that we are arises with our thoughts.
> With our thoughts, we make the world.
> Speak or act with an impure mind
> And trouble will follow you.

and he cites Ellis, Frank, Kelly, Bateson and Branden as modern exponents of some variant of this view. Cognitive therapy, then, aims to influence the manner in which a client construes reality. It challenges assumptions and beliefs and aims to achieve what Ponce, borrowing from Kuhn, terms a 'paradigm shift' in our way of perceiving the world. He goes on to argue that there are three areas of major concern to cognitive therapists: the individual's core assumptions about the nature of the *world;* the individual's core assumptions about how one ought to relate to the world; and the individual's core assumptions about the nature of the *Self.* The premise is that what brings the client into psychotherapy is some maladaptive relationship between the core assumptions and life's experience. He points out that cognitive therapists focus almost exclusively on the first two classes of assumption while taking the notion of Self as given.

Buddhism, however, offers a radical challenge to these assumptions. In particular it teaches that: (1) The world is interconnected and constantly changing (*anicca*). (2) Therefore, the only viable relationship with the world is one of non-attachment, for attachment to that which is constantly changing is doomed to frustration. (3) Therefore, attachment to a construct of Self that is separate and unchanging likewise is doomed to frustration.

Despite the claims of cognitive therapists to alter a individuals' deep assumptions concerning themselves and the world, it is doubtful whether the methods employed lead to changes sufficient to merit the description 'paradigm shift'. Indeed, Ponce joins others mentioned above in advocating Zen Buddhist methods as an integral part of therapy: '. . . meditation is a skilful device. . . to facilitate the necessary transformation of the person's world views.' He further adds that:

> Meditation very quickly demonstrates to the meditator (1) The autonomy of, and therefore the futility of controlling, his/her internal processes like thoughts, images, sensations, percepts. They seem to have a will of their own, and come and go in consciousness of their own accord; (2) The Self (I, Ego, Me, Willpower) is discovered not only to be impotent as a controlling agent of these processes, but turns out to be merely one of the numerous thought forms that flits in and out of consciousness; (3) At some point in the meditative experience the knower (subject); the known (object) and the knowing (process), become a single flowing process, obliterating separation and fragmentation. All that remains is the sound, the image, the breath, the mosquito bite. It is at this level that the world is perceived as interconnected.

In Tibetan Buddhism there is a painting known as 'The Wheel of Life', copies and versions of which are used often to portray the world view of Buddhism. Of particular relevance to the present discussion is the manner in which conscious thought is portrayed. It is represented graphically by a 'chattering monkey': as monkeys leap from branch to branch, so do our thoughts leap from one subject to another. It is this 'monkey mind' that deals in the world of categories, labels, and polarised constructs and prevents us from seeing the world 'as it is', for 'when the opposites arise, the Buddhamind is lost'. When we categorise we set boundaries and limits, and so we do with our idea of Self. We tell ourselves what we are or are not able to do, what we can or cannot stand, and then we react violently, even psychotically when we have reached our 'limit'. Through Buddhist training we begin to realise that there are no limits, that the constraints are of our own construction.

Applied Behaviour Analysis

This is the application of the radical behaviourism of B.F. Skinner to the solution of practical problems, and is included here because of the undoubted importance of Skinner in psychology, because he eschews cognitive psychology, and because his position represents a radical departure from conventional notions of the Self. Skinner is also a writer who is often critised but, we suspect, read less often. He has addressed himself regularly to subjects such as the 'Self', 'awareness', 'consciousness' and 'private events'. In particular he has been especially critical of 'ghost in the machine' theorising that postulates any interior entity that, for example, 'thinks', 'remembers', 'plans', or 'solves problems'.

> I have found it necessary from time to time to attack traditional concepts which assign spontaneous control to the special inner self called the speaker. Only in this way could I make room for the alternative explanation of action which it is the business of a science of verbal behaviour to construct.

Skinner draws a clear distinction between 'mental' and 'private'. Statements about the mind either refer to a fictional explanatory construct or tun out on translation to be statements about actual behaviour. Whereas sentences about private events refer to events taking place at a covert level (toothaches, feelings, dreams, images, etc.) and that are accessible solely to the person concerned. These events, he holds, share the same status as overt behaviour and hence are subject to the same laws and principles as overt behaviour. The skin is viewed as an arbitrary boundary: feelings, emotions and thoughts are subject to the same variables that influence any other behaviour. Consciousness, thoughts, dreams, do not occupy a special world of their own, nor do they have any special casual role. They are simply more examples of ways of behaving that are amenable to explanation. The Self is, at worst, an explanatory fiction and, at best, 'a repertoire of behaviour' that has developed as a result of our interaction with our environment.

> It is often said that a science of behaviour studies the human organism but neglects the person or self. What it neglects is a vestige of animism, a doctrine which in its crudest form held that the body was moved by one or more indwelling spirits . . . Traces of the doctrine survive when we speak of a *personality*, of an ego in ego psychology, of an *I* who says he knows what he is going to do and uses his body to do it. . . A person is not an originating agent; he is a locus, a point at which many genetic and environmental conditions come together in a joint effect.

Our 'sense of Self', then, is inferred from our behaviour (as are, according to Skinner, the various 'cognitive processes' that are then studied erroneously by cognitive psychologists). And in this picture any personal growth or self-development will result from advantageous interaction with the environment.

> Measures taken to change feelings – as in 'developing the ego' or 'building a vital sense of self' – work by constructing contingencies of reinforcement, by advising a patient where favourable contigencies are to be found, or by supplying rules which generate behaviour likely to be reinforced in his daily life.

More recently, a disciple of Skinner's, Willard Day, has addressed the concept of Self specifically in terms of what it means to talk of personal growth, ego defences, a strong sense of Self, and so on. Day suggests that in self-development we are looking for a cluster of behaviours that might include greater honesty, less anxiety, appropriate assertion, self-confidence in novel situations, ease with others, and so on. His argument is that self-development is so difficult because of '. . .the almost universally destructive social environment in which the self-developing person has to live.' Self-development is therefore regarded as a process of learning to cope with, and adapt to, the difficulties of the world, a process that he concludes is not worth the effort:

> There is, of course, another alternative to the course described above, of struggling to modify people. . . This is to think seriously, as Skinner persistently urges, about changing the general characteristics of our social *environment*. . .

Skinner has presented us with a philosophy to which it is impossible to do justice in such a brief discussion. Nevertheless, it is not clear from radical behaviourist writings what the implications are for the individual of giving up the illusion of the Self to which Skinner refers, or indeed to what extent one should do so. Furthermore, it would seem that radical behaviourists create their own limits by bowing so deferentially to the authority of the environment. And by operating strictly within a scientific framework they '. . .can never expect to reach the Self, however much they desire to. They can no doubt talk a great deal *about* it, and that is all they can do.'

Systems Approaches to Change

The development of a systemic view of the problems faced by individuals, families and networks of people has reflected moves in other disciplines, for example, contemporary physics in seeking descriptions of reality which highlight complexity and organisation as distinct from matter and energy. The origins of this shift in interest can be traced back to the paradigm shift in the physical sciences which occurred at the beginning of this century, although in the social sciences the change has been rather slower to find expression. Bateson offers the following comment in the context of a discussion on the usefulness of focusing on metaphors which seek to describe form as opposed to substance:

> . . .the conservative laws for energy and matter concern substance rather than form. But mental process, ideas, communication, organisation, differentiation, pattern and so on, are matters of form rather than substance.

The most widely known application of these ideas in the clinical context has been in the area of Family Therapy, which had its origins in the late 1940s and early 1950s in the United States in the work of, for example, Nathan Akerman and Murray Bowen, and more specifically in the developments spear-headed by Gregory Bateson, Jay Haley, John Weakland, Don Jackson and Milton Erikson. This work has been pursued by these and others including Salvador Minuchin, Mara Selvini Palazzoli and Paul Watzlawick.

The systemic approach to therapy and in particular the Milan approach offers a perspective which echoes the no-Self understanding described in Buddhist thought. Palazzoli and others orient the reader to their understanding in the following passages:

> . . . we must abandon the casual-mechanistic view of phenomena, which has dominated the sciences until recent times, and adopt a systemic orientation. With this new orientation, the therapist would be able to see the members of the family as elements in a circuit of interaction.

and

> Since in a systemic circuit each element interacts with totality, dichotomies, such as body-mind or conscious unconscious, lose their meaning.

With this perspective, therapists come to know that they are profoundly part of the system that they attempt to understand, and that in the process of this contact there is no injunction to distinguish between themselves and the family. Palazzoli and the Milan group, recognising this, stress the importance of live consultation and the use of a therapeutic team. This method of working maintains some difference in the family/therapist system, where difference (following Bateson) is viewed as information, and new information results in systems change, and hence behaviour change. The family's problems are those of the therapist and *vice versa*. The therapist becomes part of the informational flow which constitutes the family's reality.

However, the paradox of no-Self is that it appears in the context of Self. How should the therapist therefore understand and explain to himself the way in which he is *not* part of the family? Salvador Minuchin offers the following explanation in discussing the complementarity between Self and no-Self:

> If this. . .is carried to family therapy, the self is seen as both whole and a part of a whole–'both a particle and a wave'. Which aspects it shows depend on the situation. In individual experience, the focus is on the individual as a whole. But when the complementary aspects of the self become parts of a whole, the other parts of the whole, which also are discrete entities, are seen as affecting the behaviour and experience of all parts. Beyond the parts, there appears a new entity; an organism multibodied and purposeful, whose parts are regulated by the rules of the whole.

The systemic perspective has subtlely altered the way of understanding the individual in the therapeutic context, so that history has a different meaning, and need not be differentiated from the present in the patient's report. When using a systemic framework, memories are more clearly understood to be related to the totality of the person's experience, and not contained separately and distinctly. To be unaware of the past is the same as being unaware in the present. To be more aware of the present is to be more aware of the past.

Concluding, Minuchin offers a pithy view of how it is that the family unit is a useful system with which to work:

> Sociologists remain too distant from the specific reality of the individual, addressing themselves only to the homogenised reality of the institution; individual theorists get stuck in the tremendous idiosyncratic complexities with which an individual transacts in context. And both approaches may lose the rhythm of the dance.

No-self and the Therapist

> To dedicate oneself to the salvation of others with the conviction that there exist others who need saving is as much a source of bondage as to devote oneself to the task of one's own liberation under the impression that one has a real self to be liberated.

A glance at any psychology text will reveal that a considerable effort has been expended on defining the concept of Self. In the process of producing a more and more refined view, however, the possibility that Self is merely a hypothetical construct has been obscured. The unquestioning acceptance of this construct is misleading in that it leads to the construction of intervening variables between life/existence 'as it is' and the awareness of that experience. There is a certain irony about the way in which we attempt to develop models which are increasingly flexible and elegant constructions of what is, but by their very existence stand in the path of direct experience. Yet there is a further paradox, and that is that it appears that in order to communicate this, it is first necessary to have a model to reject.

What do 'I' mean by this concept of Self, and how should 'I' be located and understood in the context of therapy and social intercourse? In the social context of information exchange with a fellow human being, it is possible to identify two organisms, and in so far as Self refers to and is coterminous with the biological organism, the Self cannot exist. However, in the process of information exchange, it is not things which are exchanged, but ideas, and for this reason it is not necessary to make a distinction between two people. The two individuals constitute a system in which information is in circuit.

It is possible to examine the circuit at any point, for example, by focussing on the mind of one of the participants. However in any open system there is a continuous process of modification, although there will be some difference in the extent to which this enters the conscious awareness of the two people. Unless 'I' am aware of how each verbal and non-verbal cue alters my perception 'I' am not in a position to know how 'I' am being influenced, and because it may be impossible to be aware of all this information it becomes necessary to accept that the work of analysis and comprehension is 'being done for me' in the processes that constitute thinking, feeling, knowing and doing in a relationship with another. 'I' must always remain on the map, and never in the territory.

Thus, in the context of an exchange between two people, two 'Is', the concept of no-Self arises through the punctuation of the act of communication by the participator/observer. It lies in the recognition that in a totally open exchange there is no attempt to preserve a particular position, other than the position that it is more useful to communicate information freely. In order to have an open exchange, therapists must be open to new information: it is important that they do not feel trapped into defending a particular viewpoint. They communicate with the other person in an immediate fashion.

They trust that they will make the only response that they can in the circumstances. This is not meant to imply that they have no obligation to learn, but that they should accept that they will not always be able to account for the words that they are about to speak, the action they are about to do. And the urge to explain itself constitutes an attempt to reify a self-concept.

Therapists should be prepared to act into the unknown and wait to see what the consequence of that action is. As soon as they have some notion of what to expect, then they have begun to build a concept of Self, because the act of making a distinction in the world in the hope of rendering it predictable, means that 'I' begin to operate on the basis of what 'I' *assume* to be rather than what *is*. Therapists should strive to 'remember' that in solving any problem, in interacting with the world, they know the best answer without recourse to a distinct and separate decision-making process. This issue is crucial in the client/therapist relationship. Whilst the therapist strives for predictability based on the hypothetical construct of Self, 'I' impose my meaning on the client's behaviour. Where the therapist operates as no-Self then, paradoxically, 'I' validate every behaviour of the client because there is no 'I' to intervene and interpret.

How can no-Self be operationalised in therapy? What would the observer notice about someone operating according to these principles? In the client-centred therapy of Carl Rogers, something of this sort appears to be indicated when he writes 'But when this same client has come to accept deeply the fact that 'I am what I am', then she can be spontaneous and can lose her self-consciousness. In a client-centred approach one of the key concepts used to describe the relationship is 'unconditional acceptance', and this may relate in part to what is here described as operating with no-Self. However, it is not clear how the client-centred therapist reaches this position, nor exactly how to describe the therapist's position. The reason for this may be that what is going on in therapy is still construed in terms of the two individuals: the therapist and the client. Thus, while this view is one description or punctuation, it restricts itself to an 'either/or' understanding: either the client or the therapist. Where the no-Self understanding operates there is room for both 'both/and' and 'either/or' descriptions of relationships. It is not necessary to identify a client and a therapist.

The process of therapy is redefined so that there are no experts, only people exchanging information and partaking in a mutual sharing and learning activity. Until therapists are clear that there is no mission to save the client, they will strive to rescue the 'sick' person and, from the point of view of systemic thinking, become one of the elements in the connecting pattern which maintains the problem. This problem remains whilst we continue to work as therapists, and there is no easy answer to the question of how we redefine our role so that we can be seen to be doing something different from attempting to 'cure sick people'.

Coping without Self

The majority of psychotherapies act, directly or indirectly, to improve clients' self-image, and to strengthen their concept of Self rather than eliminate it. Indeed, it may be thought that this can only be so, for how else could one cope with daily life without some distinction between Self and Other? May points out that the development of self-image is generally regarded by personality theorists to be one of the most important processes in childhood, especially in the West where the strength of this self-image is highly regarded.

Writing from a predominantly Christian perspective, May observes that it is frequently later in life that some form of 'spiritual awakening' occurs, and that it is as if the whole process is repeated in reverse: 'Now what is needed is not heroic mastery but the simplicity of becoming as a little child; not self-determination but self-surrender; not self-assertion but dying to self.' This second process is made more difficult by the first, so is it necessary to develop a sense of Self? Are those with 'weak ego strength' more aware spiritually? Is the psychotic closer to experiencing 'that which is?' The answer is that it is necessary to develop a healthy ego before one can relinquish it; it is necessary to develop a strong sense of Self (or more specifically, a strong *positive* sense of Self) before surrender to Sèlf. It is necessary to learn how to cope with living in the world before we can become 'experts in living'.

The writings of Buddhists, in particular Zen Buddhists, are often dramatic, having an almost magical feel to them, but what is emphasised less often is that the process of Zen training is never ending and often arduous. Most of us will spend much of our lives striving to achieve a healthy ego, a strong sense of Self, with perhaps occasional moments of real understanding. Krynicki puts it thus: 'those experiences of oneness. . . tend to wax and wane, and become balanced by some sense of separateness. Zen practitioners tend to have a 'double orientation'. That is, they are oriented not only to the experiential world of union (which has been most emphasised in writings on Zen) but also to the experiential world of separateness. They are not stuck in a chaotic world of self/ object blurring, as is the psychotic.' The process is not dichotomous: as we continue in our training we become less egocentric, and increasingly more attuned to the feelings and needs of others. And it is this that is perhaps of most importance to the psychotherapist – to be able to see our clients more 'as they are' and less through the blinkers of our own theories and preconceptions.

Concluding Remarks

Theories can serve a valuable function for the psychotherapist. They can act as a means with which to organise and make sense of the information we receive from and about our clients. Their function is to guide and to serve as a useful tool. Furthermore, it is important to develop as cohesive a theory as possible: swinging, monkey-like, from one theoretical tree to another will produce muddled thinking. But theories can outgrow their importance, so that we start to see only that which will fit into our theoretical framework, or we too eagerly set out to translate everything into our own theoretical data-language. Then theories act to constrain rather than facilitate, to distort our perception and appreciation of that which is. And so it is with a sense of Self. It is a useful construct, one that acts as a helpful tool in the daily business of living. But it too can outgrow its importance, and then we become constrained by the boundaries of this 'theoretical construct' and the information we receive from the world is distorted to fit the theory. It is liberation from this contraint that is of no little concern to client and psychotherapist alike.

13

APPLICATIONS OF BUDDHISM IN MENTAL HEALTH CARE

Introduction

An increasing number of psychologists and members of related professions such as psychiatry and nursing are becoming interested in the potential Buddhism might have for both the practitioner and the recipient in the caring process. It is the intention of the present discussion to explore those aspects of Buddhist theory and practice which may prove valuable to those who work directly in the care and welfare of others. This theme will form the first part of the chapter. Whilst the focus will be mainly upon mental health care, many of the points raised are appropriate to other helping professions also, for example, general nursing, social work and education. In the second part two pilot projects, one in the area of mental health care and the other on training of helping professionals will be described.

The Buddhist Approach to Mental Health

To begin with it is worth restating that the task of Buddhism is first to understand the nature of suffering in its various forms and then to apply methods which step by step alleviate and eventually completely eliminate all suffering and states of dissatisfaction. Such a panoramic view of human potential lies somewhat beyond the scope of Western views of personality and therapy. However, within this panorama Buddhism does touch modern approaches towards the care of others directly and it is to these issues that we shall now turn.

A position central to Buddhist psychology is the view that the root causes of human unhappiness and dissatisfaction lie within individuals' firmly held attitudes and beliefs about themselves. For convenience these self-cognitions may be referred to as the self-image and in Buddhist terms a person's well-being is directly bound to the fluctuating fortunes of this sense of 'self' or 'I'. Buddhist theory would propose that individuals will become psychologically vulnerable to the extent to which they identify with their self-image and to the extent to which the self-image serves to overshadow the full range of personal experience.

The implication here is crucial to the contribution of Buddhist psychology to the helping professions. According to the Buddhist view our self-image is distinguishable from what has been described as our natural state of mind and qualities of this natural state are warmth, openness and intelligence. Mind is regarded as essentially pure and has been defined in Tibetan Buddhism as 'clear, formless cognising'. Given the appropriate methods the mind is potentially purifiable and the conventional mind, clouded by the processes of self-grasping, ignorance and the self-cherishing attitude, is merely in a state of transitory turbulence and distortion.

The self-image may be considered to consist of two principal processes, namely the self-cherishing thought or attitude (Tibetan: *bdag-gces 'dzin*), and self-grasping (Tibetan: *bdag 'dzin ma-rig-pa*), sometimes referred to as ego-grasping or self-grasping ignorance. Buddhists regard these as the two main threats to psychological health and well-being against which strategies are to be developed in the practical work described below.

The self-cherishing attitude refers to the strong phenomenological experience of 'I' or 'me' as typified when, for example, we are under emotional threat or embarrassment, which may evoke a strong sense of tightness or holding in the area of the chest. Such an experience is the self-cherishing attitude par excellence! However, this may be regarded as an extreme instance of the general condition which pervades most people, though sustained extremes in self-cherishing would, from the Buddhist viewpoint, tend to typify the mental disorders found in anxiety states and depression. In his book *Meaningful to Behold* Geshe Kelsang Gyatso, a highly realised meditation master and teacher, states that 'All the tearful aspects of *samsara*, from the greatest down to the smallest, arise from the self-cherishing attitude.'

The second process, namely self-grasping, is the principal subject under investigation in Buddhism. Self-grasping (or ego-grasping) has been defined as 'the compulsion, arising from ignorance, to regard one's own personality or 'I' as permanent, unchanging and existing self-sufficiently, independent of all other phenomena and the process of conceptual imputation'.

This self-grasping tendency then generates the solid base upon which the self-cherishing attitude depends. Buddhist enquiry strongly challenges the widely held assumption of an inherently existent self, as it challenges the status and nature of all phenomena. Such a view is deemed to be 'ignorant' or lacking in wisdom and is considered to be the root delusion and primary cause of all suffering. Why is it considered to be the root delusion? Simply put, where there is no self there is no sufferer. The construction by our psychological apparatus of a solid inherently existent self is considered in Buddhism to be a fundamental distortion of reality which gives rise to a wide range of psychophysiological consequences, one example of which is a state of extreme vulnerability to changing circumstances which may culminate in mental disorder or physical ill-health.

Such a distortion of perception gives rise to a deeply held dualistic and dis-integrated view of self and other and as such may be considered to underlie mental states which range from the ambitious drive for worldly power to the confusion and incoherence of psychosis. Buddhist psychology regards the issue of errant perception of self to be so crucial that one may describe all of its practices as in some way having a bearing upon this problem.

From this central error, secondary distortions, delusions, are likely to arise and these include craving/desire, aversion/ anger, pride/arrogance and jealously. If self-grasping forms the container or flask of ignorance then the self-cherishing attitude may be likened to the malevolent genie rising from it.

This view of self-cherishing as troublemaker has a long history in Tibetan Buddhist practice. Earlier Tibetan practitioners have called it the 'devil with the head of an owl': monks and nuns may throw up their hands in dismay when it manifests in their heart and it has been described in the Tibetan Thought Training tradition (see below) as 'the one object of every blame, deserving to be banished'.

The problem of self-cherishing is most effectively tackled through the development of its principle antidote, namely love and compassion, whereby the narrow self-boundaries associated with self-cherishing are widened through empathic involvement with others.

Traditional Approaches to the Problems of Self-cherishing

The methods of working within mental health care described here are based mainly upon traditional teachings given by Geshe Kelsang Gyatso and other eminent lamas over a period of several years. An appreciation of the traditional lineage of such methods of working with the mind is important, especially during these still pioneering days, as any attempt to abstrace certain seemingly useful methods will inevitably distort the appreciation of a subtle and complex whole. So a brief description of this background is in order.

The traditional works upon which the described methods are based include principally the *Bodhisattvacharyvatara* (*Guide to the Bodhisattva's Way of Life*) by Shantideva, the basis for Geshe Kelsang Gyatso's commentary and the *Seven Point Thought Transformation* by Geshe Chekawa. It is salutory for present day therapists to consider that Shantideva lived in the eighth century and Geshe Chekawa in the twelfth.

There are two established strategies for tackling the self-cherishing attitude. One is known as the 'Six causes and one effect', the other 'Exchanging self with others'. However, an essential preliminary to both approaches is the practice of equanimity, that is the development of an unbiased attitude towards all beings. For example, by analysing deeply the basis of our positive and negative conceptions of people we may discover that our belief that some individuals are always positive and others negative is a distortion. Over time some 'friends' may become 'strangers' or even 'enemies', while we may become friends in the future with someone who presents us with difficulties and problems at present. In worldly existence everything is changing, relationships come and go, develop and decline in a continual flux. Our dearest child today was an unknown entity to us prior to their birth and may become a problematic young adult tomorrow.

This perspective then forms the basis for the first of the six causes, which is to consider that we have had and continue to have a close relationship with all beings and forms of life. In essence one feels that all beings have been a 'mother' to us and as such have cared for us and have been kind of us.

Clearly such a view sits more easily within a culture where reincarnation is an indigenous belief and where mothers are traditionally revered. However, the psychological power of such an outlook is to make us profoundly aware of the positive effects others have upon us, many of whom will be complete strangers. We can begin to notice, for example, the complex interdependence of life on this planet and the contributions of other humans and animals in providing us with food, shelter, warmth and so on. Similarly a more balanced appraisal of the continuous care which most of us have received since infancy would be considered to be fruitful.

This recollection of the kindnesses, direct or indirect, which we have received from others comprises the second cause, namely, 'remembering the kindness of all sentient beings'. Within such a positive frame of mind a practitioner will naturally initiate the third cause leading to the 'awakening mind of *bodhicitta*', the development of the strong wish to repay this kindness.

This gives rise to the fourth and fifth causes, 'the development of affectionate love' and 'the development of great compassion'. Gyatso states that the development of affectionate love towards all beings will develop naturally as a result of meditating for a long time on the first three causes. A sign of such development is to spontaneously feel heart-felt love towards anyone and not merely to those who are nearest and dearest.

The fifth cause, the development of great compassion, again is considered to arise naturally when we contemplate the sufferings of those we care for. To appreciate their problems, difficulties and so on leads easily to the generation of great compassion, the strong wish that they be free of suffering.

Then because of the depth of feeling for all people and for all life the aspirant will personally feel powerfully committed to act to alleviate others of their distress and suffering. This stage forms the sixth cause leading to the principal effect of the meditation, namely the complete abandonment of the self-cherishing attitude and the evocation of the awakening mind of *bodhicitta*. One may note that not only is the self-cherishing attitude eventually abandoned through such successful training and contemplation but also leads in Buddhist terms to the development of the realisation that the capacity to benefit others completely can only be achieved if one becomes enlightened oneself.

The second strategy or antidote to self-cherishing is the practice of exchanging self with others. In some ways this method is regarded as being a somewhat more subtle and more powerful practice than the first.

In exchanging self with others the trainees will, initially *via* the process of meditative imagination, psychologically identify themselves with an acquaintance. In so doing they will immerse themselves in that person's qualities, hopes, fears, etc. and may actually view their 'former' self from this other perspective. This is considered helpful in empathising with others' psychological distortions or delusions (for example, jealously, anger, craving, etc.) thereby facilitating the development of compassion. Several different examples may be taken and rehearsed, rather as in social skills training, and then applied in daily situations. Gradually, over time, the psychological centre of gravity of the motivated practitioner will begin to shift from 'self' to 'other'. In this way not only will mundane preoccupations with 'self' be discouraged but empathy and compassion will develop providing the basis for love – the active wish for others to be happy.

Supportive strategies for the successful development of this practice are available. One has already been mentioned: aspiring *bodhisattvas* strive to develop a strong sense of equality between themselves and others. To this may be added the suggestion to contemplate and appreciate that all beings without exception do not want suffering and do want happiness. Thus, all beings are equal and are in the same plight of having to face recurring suffering and therefore are deserving of our compassion and love.

As we are in the same predicament as the great majority of living beings, we also are worthy of our own love and care. This raises the important point that love towards oneself is not the same as the self-cherishing attitude. In Buddhist terms true love towards oneself is the antithesis of self-cherishing, in that effective concern for one's well-being leads to the taking of steps to weaken the attitude of self-cherishing.

An additional important supporting strategy for this practice is the sustained reflection upon the negative consequences of self-cherishing. As already mentioned all negative experiences are laid at the door of the self-cherishing attitude whether it be craving or the desire for circumstances to be different, or irritation/anger at what befalls us, or fear and anxiety over loss, death, or whatever. All misfortune is considered to begin and end with the self-cherishing mind.

The central point, then, in the Buddhist perspective is to appreciate that conventional approaches to well-being only serve to sustain the self-cherishing attitude and as such only serve to perpetuate the primary cause(s) of suffering.

Practice may also be assisted by observing a model of a *bodhisattva's* love either through the personal example of a qualified teacher, or by likening it to the love a parent has for their only child. Such a love is clearly very intense and the *bodhisattva* may be described as having far more love for each being than we have for ourselves. This commitment to others then serves the practitioner in two ways which may be relevant to professional helpers. The problems inherent in a narrow self-absorbed view are placed in abeyance for both practitioner and client and energy becomes available for benefitting others.

This process can be enhanced further through the practice called Taking and Giving (Tib. *Tong len*). This highly regarded practice requires the trainee to develop an intention to willingly and joyfully relieve others of their suffering. Such an intention can be fostered by visualising the suffering and difficulties of others as black smoke which aspirants, in their imagination, inhale, and experience as dissolving their own self-cherishing process or attitude, usually considered to be located at the heart. Then, from this heartfelt sense of spaciousness arises, in the form of white light, all the temporal and spiritual energy and wisdom which others need, thereby releasing them from their suffering. Following sufficient practice such a perspective begins to manifest in everyday life by willingly and happily taking on others problems etc.

Therefore, whatever problems or difficulties arise in one's own life or in the lives of those with whom we have relationships, one may take the psychological initiative by enthusiastically utilising adversity in order to become free of self-cherishing. The skill in this approach lies in the apparent paradox that the very circumstances which are conventionally likely to evoke unhappiness, frustration or whatever, can actually provide the impetus for dissolving the root of all problems.

An interesting offshoot of the practice of Taking and Giving lies in its use in Tibetan culture in the treatment of physical illness and as such was known as the 'leprosy dharma. Such an application derives from the Buddhist view that physical illness derives ultimately from the psychological distortions surrounding the processes of self-grasping and self-cherishing. Taking and Giving may be similarly recommended for dealing with personal problems of a psychological nature.

Applications of Traditional Practices within a Modern Setting

The outlines above present some of the frameworks available for tackling self-cherishing. Next to be considered is how such strategies may be utilised within a modern Western setting.

Buddhist teachers can be very skilful in illustrating how novices may put such principles into practice. For instance Sogyal Rinpoche in a talk given in 1985 advised that one could try regarding one's own suffering, difficulties and so on with an attitude of kindness. Also the nature of the experience of suffering itself may be transformed by regarding it as being light or cotton wool-like in nature, rather than the more typical experience of denseness or heaviness.

Through such practice one's mind becomes identified with the actual antidote to self-cherishing whilst the suffering itself becomes more peripheral. Also the subjective experience of love and compassion is more open than the tight sense of 'I' which often arises during suffering and it is this open, even boundless, state which Buddhist psychology regards as being more naturally valid. (When working with clients or patients with tendencies toward self-deprecation, attempts to diminish self-cherishing may merely intensify self-hatred, in which case it may prove worthwhile to use the 'kindness towards one's own suffering' approach. Such a gradual approach may be more effective than attempting a full blown commitment to love oneself.)

This simple advice, by invoking the antidotes of loving-kindness and wisdom (or valid perception) for the problems of self-cherishing and self-grasping, integrates the two main practices in the *mahayana* tradition of developing the awakening mind of love and compassion (*bodhicitta*) together with the practice of wisdom (*prajna*).

The development of kindness in the face of suffering can be extended to fully making friends with oneself, regarded as an essential prerequisite to the development of love for others. Therefore the 'equanimity meditation' in which the meditator visualises groups of individuals within the three broad categories of 'friends', 'strangers' and 'enemies' can be developed to include a visualised image or at least an impression of oneself within the array.

This practice – learning to actively regard oneself as 'just another human being' – can serve to ground oneself in one's own reality, and thus help to abandon unrealistic expectations. If in addition to developing a more balanced perception the meditator is also training in loving-kindness, for example, by imaging sending out feelings of warmth to others, it may prove therapeutic to direct such feelings towards oneself as well. Several times in workshops individuals who found it easy to feel warm and positive towards images of their own children discovered they were blocked when attempting to generalise a similar feeling towards an image of themselves.

Positive attitudes towards those who cause us difficulties are also problematic. The Tibetan traditions place considerable emphasis upon the role which an 'enemy' or similar negative individual may have upon our spiritual development. For example, His Holiness the Dalai Lama has often stated that 'our enemy is our greatest teacher.' To develop love for those whom we care for is rather different from loving our antagonist. But psychologically there is considerable benefit to be obtained by working on the development of loving-kindness towards those who regard us negatively. One strategy for achieving this is to appreciate that those who disregard us are in actuality suffering themselves. Patients may be perceived as suffering from their condition rather than specifically attacking us. This may provide some psychological space for the helper wherein a more positive, balanced and mutually beneficial state of mind may arise.

Buddhist practice fosters a constructive outlook upon adversity in general. That such an attitude is not merely a 'rosy outlook' or 'putting a brave face on things' can be appreciated by the fact that an essential part of Buddhist training is to deeply consider the drawbacks of general existence until what is known as 'the mind of definite emergence'.develops which vigorously seeks a solution to such difficulties.

Skilful practitioners have several options available when faced with any form of adversity. They may be reminded of the shortcomings of worldly existence; may choose to practise patience, an essential quality in the control of anger; choose to contemplate the causally dependent consequences of previous unskilful actions (*karma*) or may use the situation to work upon the self-chershing attitude through the practice of Taking and Giving.

The problems of anger can be tackled in various ways. As an example the Dalai Lama has described anger as a loss of courage, so that the practice of patience becomes an act of bravery, of not being pushed into anger. In the practice of mindfulness, thoughts or feelings of anger may be merely observed and allowed to pass. Other approaches include using the energy of anger positively and creatively, or merely to regard oneself as an inert block of wood when provoked.

The world view implicit in a spiritual tradition or culture may subtly influence therapeutic work. For instance the Buddhist teacher Chogyam Trungpa, recalling his observations upon coming to the West some twenty years ago, was struck by the pervasive world view of guilt and the notion or 'original sin' which carried with it the feeling that present misfortune was in some way a punishment for a mistake in the past. A subtle difference between this view and the Buddhist perspective of *karma* would be the tendency, found in Western therapies such as psychoanalysis, to over-emphasise the past and be somewhat 'backward looking'. Perhaps in Western psychology the approaches of Rogers, Maslow and Fromm come closer to the Buddhist view, particularly with respect to the emphasis upon developing positive regard for oneself. If all beings possess 'buddha nature' there is no merit in guilt or self-deprecation, which from a Buddhist viewpoint can appear quite ludicrous.

The twin attack outlined so far on self-grasping and self-cherishing may lead to more positive functioning, being more in touch with reality and without typical distortions of perception and feeling. High levels of psychological well-being then would tend to be associated with low levels of self-cherishing whilst low levels of psychological well-being and mental disorder in the Buddhist view would be identified with high levels of self-cherishing. Instances of the latter are readily identifiable in cases where the individual's self-image tends to be ineffectual or incapacitating, such as various anxiety states. One may note though that Buddhist psychology would tend to describe anyone with high levels of self-cherishing as being mentally disordered irrespective of their apparent success in the world.

The themes discussed so far suggest that Buddhist theory and practice may be equally appropriate for both practitioner and client. Such an orientation is to be found in the Maitri project in Colorado, USA. This extremely interesting venture is an application of the principles of Tibetan Buddhism to the problems of mental disorder. Founded by Chogyam Trungpa, Maitri is a therapeutic community wherein both therapists and patients are essentially realising their own human potential through living and working with each other. Within such a context the term 'neurosis' could be applied to anyone in the community, whether staff or patient, since from a Buddhist view any unenlightened person may be regarded as being in some way neurotic. Through living in such a way any therapist would have opportunities to mount an assault upon self-cherishing and in so doing expand their own self-boundaries.

Additionally, both therapists and patients would be practising the development of mindfulness and gaining an appreciation of the workings of their mind through sitting meditation. (For those patients for whom sitting meditation is inappropriate, alternative and more active practices have been developed.) The Maitri project then provides a practical example of how the traditional principles of *bodhicitta* training may be implemented within a modern setting.

If our aim is to become psychologically healthy and to have clear and undistorted perception, then the Buddhist advice to helping professionals and their clients would be to know your own mind! This task of knowing the mind takes as its foundation the practice of mindfulness (*satipatthana*), which is to be found in all traditions of Buddhism. To be mindful is to be fully aware in the present and mindfulness is a highly regarded practice in its own right as well as being an essential prerequisite for many other practices. Even a brief taste of this practice will reveal its therapeutic benefits and potential. Its simplicity reveals its purity and there is no need for religious trappings. A common form of the practice is to concentrate on the breath entering and leaving the nostrils, and the difficulty experienced in attempting to follow this practice for any period of time reveals the state of our minds to us. Yet the beneficial effects of this practice may often occur quickly and relatively easily.

In addition to being useful to both client and practitioner as a stress-reduction technique, Deatherage has described several ways in which mindfulness training may be incorporated into clinical practice. For example, one patient with poor concentration was asked to practice looking at the second hand of an electric clock. Another, preoccupied with thoughts from the past was asked to apply the lebel 'remembering, remembering' when she discovered herself having such thoughts during the day. And a third example was of a young woman, clinically considered to be 'unfeeling', who was instructed to try breathing meditation and also requested to note any emotion that might arise and interrupt attention to her breathing. This led to the discovery of a wide range of strong feelings which apparently had been previously outside of awareness.

Whilst many subtle processes may be noted during sitting meditation, valuable clinical material can arise if a patient attempts to become more mindful of their psychological processes when engaged in daily life. From this procedure some 'distance' arises within the mind which facilitates disentanglement from psychological turmoil. Whilst a

Buddhist view may ultimately question the nature and status of a 'self' that observes, to be able to stand back from personal emotional dramas is a valued psychological development.

The above examples parallel my own pilot work. During 1979 - 81 a series of self-awareness groups were started at St. Crispin's hospital, Northampton. The first two groups were conducted with psychiatric staff, the third and fourth with patients. The staff groups involved about ten people in each group, comprising clinical psychologists, consultant psychiatrists, mental nurses and psychiatric social workers. Nurse members of the groups varied according to shift rotation.

The aims of these self-awareness groups were stated as follows: 'To find out the extent to which individual control and awareness can be increased in our responses to situations and others. The more we increase our sense of well-being the more energy is available for benefitting others.'

Exercises were practised for a period of one hour, once a week in a group setting. The following exercise may serve as an example: 'Observe and note your own thoughts from time to time as you go about your daily activities. Whilst doing this try not to hold on to the thoughts. Just identify them. Are your thoughts more concerned with the past, present or future? Just note 'past', 'present', 'future' By way of linking the self-awareness sessions to other therapeutic approaches established within the hospital, principally behaviour therapy and social skills training, empathy and compassion were presented as skills capable of development and refinement.

One exercise on empathy required group members to visualise a patient in mental distress and then to notice their own reactions to the needs of their patients. They were then asked whether they felt able to really help them. The next stage was to visualise actually being able to help. Again staff were asked to note how they reacted to such change. The exercise was extended to explore how empathy was affected by disappointment as when for example they met the above patient the following day only to find that he or she had relapsed. Again they were to be aware of how they responded. The exercise could be extended to include several stages of improvement and deterioration.

To cope positively with such fluctuation seems to correspond with the Buddhist training which integrates loving-kindness with patience. Trungpa speaks of developing the quality of fearlessness, of being open with others and their neuroses yet never giving up on them. He states 'If you have patience with people, they slowly change. You do have some effect on them if you are radiating your sanity. They will begin to take notice, although of course they don't want to let anybody know.'

Bearing in mind the demands made upon staff it became evident during the group sessions that many staff would benefit from nurturing a more positive attitude towards themselves. Part of this process of 'making friends' with oneself meant avoiding treating ourselves more harshly than we do others. Whilst we might force-feed ourselves with junk food when pressed for time we would rarely adopt the same attitude towards colleagues. A clear instance of such harshness would be an intolerance towards any less than perfect performance.

In the lives of the staff there appeared to be a variety of frustrations from several sources. Rather than analyse any particular situation, one approach was to work with the reaction of frustration itself. Each group member was asked to imagine as vividly as possible any frustrating situation which they had recently experienced and to include as much detail as possible. The feeling of frustration was to be felt as deeply as possible including all of its physical and mental aspects.

Next they were asked to just label or note this experience as it arose in imagination (that is, as frustration, tension, etc.) and to be aware of their response. This was followed by imagining that their complete response had switched from frustration to peace and relaxation. This was to be felt as fully as possible. The switch of feeling was experimented with further by going back to the feeling of frustration and thence back again.

The aim was to enable any particular individual to gain some choice and control over their emotional reactions. Such a playful attitude to what may be experienced as a heavily laden feeling may seem to be rather 'irreverent' but is in accord with Buddhist views on the potential flexibility which we have in our reactions to situations. Staff were also encouraged to generalise strategies from the group to the work setting.

The attitude of staff towards this venture was on the whole one of cooperation. They were forthcoming, warm and welcomed a change in their daily routine. Only one member of the two groups stated that they felt sceptical about the motivation behind having such group sessions.

Of the various exercises used those which seemed most appropriate and interesting to staff were the labelling and noting of one's own experience, especially of negative and unwanted states; changing one's perception of others by becoming more positive and seeing how this affected one's own behaviour; and experimenting with feeling compassion for oneself and again observing the consequences of feeling more relaxed and so on when with others.

Visualisation as a learning method requires practice, so in the exercises emphasis was placed more on 'sensing' a particular situation than on visual detail. Subjective reports suggested that well-being could be influenced in the initial sessions even with rather rough visualisation skills. The methods do require rehearsal on a daily basis along with reinforcement in daily situations for well-being, flexibility and empathy to become increasingly rewarding. Staff did mention that they considered such training to be useful for any helping professional.

On the basis of the work carried out with the staff groups it was proposed to introduce broadly the same range of exercises to two groups of long stay patients in a rehabilitation ward. Some of these patients were in the stage of preparing to move into flat-type accommodation, firstly in the hospital and then in the community. Their programme was wide ranging and included social skills groups, psychodrama and occupational therapy.

Given the situation of the patients it was felt appropriate, after consultation with a senior clinical psychologist, to apply those Buddhist practices which emphasised calmness, mindfulness and positive social attitudes (that is, the *bodhicitta* type of training). Two main aims were to help patients cope with the variety of circumstances likely to occur outside of the hospital setting and to facilitate rapport with others. Therefore, the focus was very similar to that of the staff groups with exercises being selected to foster greater personal autonomy and well-being in the face of changing circumstances, and to develop more positive social attitudes towards others. Given that each group met for the self-awareness session only one hour each week emphasis was laid upon the need for practice in daily settings inside and outside the hospital. Nurse staff on the wards were also encouraged to remind the patients to do some of the exercises, such as mindfulness and relaxation, when they were in their rooms.

Attention and concentration were clearly a difficulty. One approach was to ask each patient to bring in something that could serve as an object of concentration. The exercise took the form of attending to details of the object, say an ornament. After a few minutes of observation patients would describe the object to each other. In this way both motivation and sustained attention to detail could develop. Also, when back, in their rooms patients could use the objects again in exercises on concentration. Another possibility was to suggest to patients that they spend a few minutes a day developing concentration by attending to the second hand of a clock. Emphasis upon training in the conscious control of attention was also linked with increasing positive perceptions in general. Positive qualities in fellow patients, oneself or staff could be perceived more consciously and reinforced. Also, warmer feelings in general might be nurtured which could shift a person's psychological 'centre of gravity' away from the self-cherishing attitude.

Some examples may be of interest. One patient suffered from a stream of self-deprecating thoughts and was overwhelmed with thoughts of the past. He claimed no compassion, no enjoyment in life, and was full of self-hatred. Upon practising mindfulness breathing for a few minutes with the instruction to just note those thoughts and distractions which may arise he reported some relief and peace. As well as verbally reporting that he felt better, the patient did appear calmer and more collected. The suggestion was also made that he try to recall positive acts which occurred in daily situations. However, by the end of the session the patient would often be as restless as before.

One amusing comment by another patient doing the same exercise was 'This reminds me of Buddhist meditation'. Apparently her daughter had previously introduced the same method to her. In her case, the mindfulness practice led to an enhanced awareness of her predominant emotional state: fear of leaving the hospital. The fear was tackled through the development of warmth and compassion towards oneself and others, along with learning to perceive others as non-threatening. As this woman had faith in God and loved nature, these attitudes were encouraged as sources of nourishment for her.

A third example was a male patient, who like most of the others was in his late forties or fifties. He responded very well to the empathy type of training where one rehearsed sending out feelings of warmth and caring to others. This was helped by considering that all people have problems and difficulties, including staff, and do not want suffering. He made an effort to generalise from the group sessions to the occupational therapy section where he had a supervisory role. This was supported by discussing the interdependent structure of a hospital and the general environment.

About eighteen months after the first series of awareness groups it was proposed that a team consisting of a senior clinical psychologist, psychiatric social worker and myself develop the exercises so that they might be integrated with cognitive problem solving strategies. This time most of the patients were female and short-stay. Occasionally other patients, including one or two men, would join the group.

Sessions were to be one hour long, twice weekly, over twelve weeks. Again this was to be a pilot exploration working with new approaches rather than monitoring specific changes in patients.

A similar range of exercises was used as in the earlier groups with emphasis upon relaxation and concentration, the development of empathy and warmth towards oneself and others, together with training in the choice and direction of emotional responses. The exercises were to be alternated with the cognitive problem solving sessions for the first few weeks. Progressively sessions would become shared to help patients to integrate both lines of approach. Given the differences between the two perspectives, it was considered helpful to develop common concepts as far as possible. For example, the concept of 'focussing' was introduced to describe to patients both the attention necessary to become aware of one's breathing and the attention required when rehearsing a cognitive behavioural sequence such as taking a trip to town. Both approaches might be involved in a particular behavioural sequence. Role-playing going into a shop and asking for a specific item might include focussing upon being mindful, developing positive attitudes towards self and others, plus awareness and control of feelings.

Also practised was the choice and change of emotional responses based upon approaches outline by Tarthang Tulku. He stated, 'for example, every time you think you are not happy, say, 'I am happy'. Say it strongly to yourself, even if your feelings are contradictory. Remember, it is your self-image and not you. Just as fast as a fish can move in the water, you can instantly change to a happy, balanced attitude. Keep yourself there, Believe yourself. . . You have the choice.'

This approach was used to practise changing feelings in the shop role-play by contrasting the effects of positive and friendly behaviour with a negative and withdrawn response. The aim of such rehearsal was to gain some direction and confidence over our emotional life whilst realising that we need not identify with nor be dominated by our feelings.

The range of material developed in the awareness groups was also used in the professional training of nurses and social workers and in weekend workshops for helping professionals in general. The context was a course of professional training in stress management and counselling. As with the previous groups, the emphasis was upon the mindfulness and empathy/warmth exercises. The latter included an appreciation of difficult clients/colleagues as being victims of their own psychological states. Also included was the development of choice and control over emotional reactions. The exercises were introduced in several ways. Sometimes they accompanied other awareness exercises relevant to counselling training, such as the effects of positive/negative feedback upon others. On other occasions, it was appropriate to introduce Buddhist perspectives on mental health in their own right.

It was often useful when working with self-image from a Buddhist perspective to use self-drawing techniques derived from other therapeutic approaches such as gestalt therapy. These 'self-drawings' would be more in the nature of spontaneous doodles rather than artistic constructions. In fact, from the point of view of the exercise the more intuitive and spontaneous the drawing the better. The approach used was rather similar to that used by Kubler-Ross in her work with terminally ill patients and their families.

The self-drawings would only take a few minutes to do and the interesting work occurred often when students described their drawings to others who were 'counselling' them. As in Kubler-Ross's work the great majority of people were able to do the exercise, even if initially hesitant, and the material was often extremely interesting and profound. The exercise could be extended by working with an ideal self-image through asking the question 'How I would like to be?' Comparison could be made with the present self image and links might be developed between the two. By using this method Buddhist approaches to the self can be explored and if appropriate one may use the drawings as a framework for exploring the expansion of self-boundaries. Specific delusions such as anger, fear, craving or clinging may also be explored in a similar way.

One variation of the exercise with direct bearing on the work in the psychiatric staff and patient groups was to depict the self helping others. This was often useful in that the sense of boundary between self and other could be worked with or at least observed in a topographical form. In such a way one's own fears or sense of inadequacy in relation to others may be usefully explored in terms of the boundary between self and client/patient. One might then work upon extending or dissolving this boundary to allow the flow of warmth or positive energy towards ourselves and others, rather as in the visualisation methods described above.

My own feeling is that the potential for applying the essence of Buddhist wisdom in the helping professions is considerable. Trungpa speaks of the 'basic sanity' of the spiritual traditions, and it is largely by using the techniques and ideas that these traditions offer us, as tools for self-examination, that we may hope to recapture some of the sanity that we seem to have lost.

Concluding Remarks

My aim here has been to try to demonstrate how some aspects of Buddhist knowledge and wisdom may be applied in a practical way within a clinical setting. The attitude of loving-kindness appears an excellent protection for the helping professional. Not only is it an antidote to the problems which accompany the self-cherishing attitude, thereby enabling the practitioner to become more effective and balanced, but loving-kindness also serves as a protection against the stresses of the helping relationship itself. As mentioned in the traditional practices such as Taking and Giving, the attitude of love and compassion also becomes a great source of energy.

There is an optimism in Buddhist psychology with respect to both training and counselling/therapy in that qualities such as loving-kindness can be acquired or enhanced. Therefore, the human potential of both practitioner and recipient in the helping relationship can be developed.

14

BUDDHISM AND BEHAVIOUR CHANGE : IMPLICATIONS FOR THERAPY

Few other ancient spiritual traditions have aroused greater interest and curiosity among modern psychologists and psychotherapists than Buddhism. The psychological relevance of much of Buddhist teachings had been recognised from the time the pioneering English translations of the canonical texts began to appear, a little over a century ago, under the aegis of the Pali Test Society. The popularity achieved by Zen Buddhism in the West in the last few decades both reflects and has further contributed to the interest in, and indeed the serious study of, Buddhism by Western psychologists and therapists. The common ground between the ideas and practices of Buddhism on the one hand, and those of Western psychology and psychotherapy on the other, has been discussed quite extensively. A recent issue of a Japanese psychology journal was devoted entirely to this topic.

Concepts of Therapy

In considering the relevance of the Buddhist tradition to modern psychological therapy, it is necessary to examine, briefly the concept of therapy. While in general the term 'therapy' is easily and unambiguously understood, it is important to recognise that it can be used in several senses.

Firstly, and most commonly, 'therapy' refers to a systematic attempt to put matters right when something has gone wrong with a person's health. In the context of psychological health, abnormalities or aberrations of behaviour and/or experience (such as depression, anxiety, phobias, obsessional thoughts, compulsive rituals) require correction, with standard procedures. Most practising therapists use the term 'therapy' to refer to this exercise. It is a moot point as to when to consider a behaviour or experience normal or abnormal; suffice it to say, for the present purposes, that when such a development causes interference with people's normal functioning and is thus distressing to them and/or their family and friends, it becomes a problem requiring therapy. Such problems may include, in addition to clearly unusual behaviours or experiences, deficits (for example, lack of social or communication skills) as well as excesses (for example, overeating, uncontrolled drinking). Therapy in this sense is *remedial.*

Secondly, one can conceive of therapy in a future-directed sense; that is, therapy can be *prophylactic*. Steps can be taken with the intention of preventing a dysfunction, or any other problem, from taking place. Consider, for example, counselling offered to a family with a seriously ill person. This is prophylactic therapy in that the family is being prepared, among other things, to cope with the loss that is impending. The preventive use of therapy can be aimed at warding off problems totally (for example, stress inoculation training), or at preventing a condition getting worse, or at stopping a condition or problem leading to further difficulties.

Thirdly, one can consider therapy not for what is generally recognised as a problem, but as an endeavour aimed at improving one's well-being and functioning. This can at times overlap with the first two senses of the term 'therapy', especially the second, but should be seen as conceptually distinct. For example, if we consider that normal human existence in the hectic industrialised world of today is ridden with all sorts of anxieties, worries and disappointments, and therefore an unsatisfactory state, then one might wish to take steps towards alleviating not any specific symptom or problem but the entire unsatisfactory condition, by altering one's basic responses to one's surroundings. This is particularly relevant in discussing Buddhism, as the Buddhist concept of *dukkha* (usually translated as 'suffering') presents us with just this kind of radical standpoint with regard to what we take for granted as normal existence. The aim of attempting to help people deliver themselves, *via* a process of personal development, from this unsatisfactory state is, it can be argued, broadly a therapeutic one.

Influence of Buddhism on Therapeutic Practice

The recent years have witnessed a shift in the interest of psychologists and psychotherapists in Buddhism. It is no longer purely an academic interest; it has now moved into the arena of actual clinical practice. Attempts are being made to apply, in clinical settings, what Buddhism has to offer. There is, for example, a considerable literature today on the use of various Buddhist meditational techniques for common clinical problems. Both case studies and, more importantly, controlled trials have been published showing the utility of the applications of meditation. The clinical uses of meditation as a form of psychological therapy have spread into such diverse areas as headaches, insomnia, general tension, chronic fatigue, drug abuse, excessive self-blame, pathological bereavement reactions, separation anxiety and low frustration tolerance. In Japan, not only meditation but other traditional Buddhist practices as well have begun to be systematically used in the context of psychotherapy. Professor Kishimoto, for instance, has reported on the use of what he calls 'self-awakening psychotherapy' as an essential and integral part of his therapeutic package for neurotic patients. Of particular interest in his use of the practices of the different Buddhist schools and sects or sub-schools (Rinzai-Zen and Soto-Zen of the Zen school; and Jodo and Jodo-Shin of the Jodo school) to suit each individual patient. Kishimoto has described, for example, the treatment of a seventy-eight year old housewife presenting with anxiety and compulsive neurosis, with a therapy package which included the Naikan method of meditation – this being one of the distinctive techniques associated with the Rinzai sect of Zen to which the patient belonged. Such use of traditionally-derived practices that match the belief system of the patient is beginning to gain ground in clinical practice in other settings as well. The use of the Hindu concept Karma Yoga in the behavioural treatment of a Hindu woman has been described recently by Singh and Oberhummer in the US. Such matching of therapy to patient may not be always feasible, but if judiciously used it can undoubtedly contribute to greater acceptance of and compliance with therapeutic instructions. More importantly perhaps, it can also be argued that it can turn the experience of therapy for a particular problem into a wider and more rewarding experience of personal improvement and growth, within the secure context of one's belief system.

This entry of Buddhist ideas and practices into the arena of modern psychological therapy makes it necessary to examine closely and critically, both the potential contribution Buddhism can make to therapy, and the possible ways and means of effecting this contribution in a meaningful and systematic way. Some writers have expressed the ambitious notion of developing an integrated new system, which encompasses both Buddhist and modern therapeutic ideas, while others have argued for more limited goals. In practice, what is required is the development of a rational basis for the use of Buddhist notions and practices within the context of therapy to suit each individual and each setting. Such a development will take some time and a great deal of effort to accomplish, but it remains a legitimate goal.

An essential first requirement in this exercise is to undertake a close examination of the concepts and strategies of behaviour change that are found in Buddhism. Behaviour change is, in the ultimate analysis, the most important factor in the therapeutic enterprise; this applies not only to the end product of therapy, but also, to a considerable extent, to the specific steps that are taken in the quest for that end product. After successful therapy, a person would be expected to show behaviours that are different from those prior to therapy (for example, a previously social phobic patient would be able to face social situations without fear and cope with such occasions productively). Equally, the process of therapy itself would often involve new and different response patterns (for example, a spiderphobic patient receiving exposure therapy would engage in increasingly more approach behaviours in the presence of spiders during the therapy). Behaviour change is thus of prime importance in psychological therapy.

Notions of Behaviour Change in Buddhism

Let us now examine, briefly, some of the concepts and strategies of behaviour change found in Buddhism. There are many and diverse schools and sub-schools of Buddhism, each with its own literature and tradition. In the following sections, our discussion will be confined to Early Buddhism that is, the form of Buddhism, usually called Thervada, which is contained in the canonical tests and their early commentaries in the Pali language. The canonical texts are the books of the *Tipitaka (Sutta, Vinaya and Abhidhamma)*, and the commentaries considered here are those that were in their present form by the fifth century AD. These represent the Buddha's original teachings and their elaboration and analysis by the earliest disciples and scholars within the Theravada tradition.

Attainment of Perfection : the Arahant State

Buddhism accepts that behaviour change is possible, and encourages and extols change in the right direction. Such change, in the form of personal development, is indeed essential for the main aim of the religious endeavour, which is the attainment of *Nibbana*. The ultimate personal perfection is the state of being an *arahant* ('the worthy one', 'the perfected one') and is aspired to by all Buddhists. What does it mean to say that someone is an *arahant? Arahants* are those who have extinguished the cycle of births and deaths. They have severed the cankers and fetters that bind one to the cycle of *dukkha*, or suffering. They have understood the three qualities of impermanence, suffering and selflessness that pervade all existence. An example of a short description of an *arahant* in the Canon (there are numerous such descriptions) may be cited:

> The *arahant* has destroyed the cankers, lived the life, done what was needed to be done, set down the burden, won self-weal, shattered life's fetters, and is freed by perfect knowledge. He has applied himself to six things: to dispassion, to detachment, to harmlessness, to the destruction of craving, to the destruction of grasping, and to non-delusion.

In psychological terms, *arahants'* actions no longer emanate from the common motives of greed or lust, malice and delusion, though they are capable of joy or positive sentiment. They have loving kindness (*metta*) to all, and compassion (*karuna*). They indulge in nothing, and are restrained in their behaviour. Nine standards of behaviour are given which *arahants* cannot and do not transgress (*Anguttara Nikaya*): taking life; stealing; sexual contact; uttering falsehoods; enjoying comforts of wealth; and going astray through desire, through hate, through delusion and through fear. They contribute to society by being teachers and advisors, and they are no burden to their fellow beings.

How does one reach the state of *arahant*hood, which as seen above is characterised by, among others, a certain set of behaviours and experiences? According to the texts, the actual attainment or occasion of this state is a sudden and abrupt change. There are numerous examples of disciples reaching this state while hearing the Buddha's preaching. Other examples refer to some major triggering experience which causes a significant impact on the person. For instance, in the *Theragatha*, the Elder Kulla is reported as describing his attainment of *arahant*hood when he came upon a rotting, untended and worm-infested human corpse in a field. Seeing this, he said to himself: 'Behold, the four-compound, diseased, impure, dripping, exuding – the pride of fools!' He then contemplated the corpse, relating it to his own self, and attained the *arahant* state.

Although the attainment itself is sudden, this can take place only in a person prepared and ready for the change, having gone through a process of self-development involving restraint in conduct, word and thought, and in meditation. Meditation of both the *samatha* (calm) type and the *vipassana* (insight) type are considered relevant. The texts refer to the various stages that many disciples go through, before attaining *arahant*hood. Three prior stages are described, characterising those who have made spiritual progress but not yet attained the final state (*sotapanna, sakadagami, anagami*). Those who have not reached even the first of these are the *puthujjanas:* the truly lay, or uninitiated, ones. These are, of course, the vast multitude.

It is important to emphasise that the attainment of *arahant*hood is the result of preparation and endeavour. This involves behaviour change based on restraint, and on self-development which in turn is based on meditation exercises. In short the final, global, personal change encompassed in the state of *arahant*hood is achieved by a process of systematic behaviour change as a means to it.

Specific Behaviour Changes and Strategies for Achieving Them

An even more significant point, in the present context, is that the Buddha also considered the well-being of oneself and of one's fellow-beings as an important aim in a layperson's life. This was not merely as an early prelude to the preparation for *arahant*hood, but as a goal in its own right. The Buddha preached explicitly on the need to improve the quality of one's day-to-day life. This involved restraining oneself from behaviour that harmed others, and from excesses, and conducting oneself dutifully towards one's family, neighbours, teachers, elders and others. Behaviours that were likely to lead to unhappy consequences, such as drinking alcohol, womanising and gambling, were discouraged (see, for examples, *Sigalovada Sutta of the Digha Nikaya*). The Buddhist lay ethic is a strongly pragmatic one; what is recommended is what is conducive to the individual's and others well-being. Its basis does not lie in dogma or doctrine. Alcohol abuse, for example, is discouraged on the grounds that it can lead to ill-health, loss of wealth, derangement of mind, proneness to socially unacceptable behaviours and increased quarrels.

The corollary of this position is that Buddhism recognises the importance, and the feasibility, of specific behaviour changes when and where required. This is a much-neglected aspect of Buddhism, but an extremely important one. The Buddhist concepts and strategies of behaviour change are not confined to the major spiritual training that is required in a committed religious life, with the ultimate aim of attainment of *arahant*hood, but include specific and well-defined ways of changing day-to-day behaviours as well.

Examples of such behaviour-change strategies found in early Buddhism are varied and numerous. Interestingly, some of these are not very different from the corresponding techniques used in modern behavioural psychotherapy. The Buddha and his early disciples both used and recommended such techniques where suitable. These are essentially behavioural techniques, with no recourse to insight or inner factors. They involved specific behavioural steps aimed at directly changing the response in question, in exactly the same way that modern behaviour therapy operates.

Some of these techniques found in Early Buddhism are: (1) There are numerous references to modelling as a way of influencing, and thereby modifying, the behaviour of others. (2) The principle of reciprocal inhibition, along with graded exposure, is acknowledged on at least one occasion as a fear-reduction technique. (3) The modification of undesirable habits by multiple behavioural techniques is acknowledged. The clearest case illustrating this is one of over-eating (see below). The techniques used include the graded acquisition of control over the target behaviour, use of cues, response cost, and involvement of a family member to implement the programme. The package is remarkably similar to what a modern behaviour therapist would offer for a similar problem. (4) Stimulus control as a means of eliminating undesired behaviours is mentioned. (5) The systematic use of rewards is referred to, as a means of inducing and encouraging desirable behaviours. (6) There is at least one clear account of what is best described as social skills training. (7) For the control of unwanted intrusive cognitions, several techniques are recommended which include: thought-stopping, thought-switching, distraction and overexposure. (8) Self-monitoring, by way of training in mindfulness, is advocated as a strategy for dealing with such problems as poor sleep and fears. (9) A graded stimulus approach is recommended for the development of loving kindness, much like the hierarchical approach used in many modern behavioural strategies. (10) A strategy very similar to covert sensitisation is used for both the control of unwanted thoughts and for controlling and eliminating lust and attachment. (11) Several cognitive and cognitive-behavioural methods are also found, including the use of parable and analogy, and the repeated exposure to disconfirmatory experiences in dealing with false beliefs, not unlike some of the strategies of modern cognitive therapies.

For reasons of space, we shall not discuss the above in any detail here. Fuller accounts of these, and of their clear similarity to modern behaviour therapeutic techniques, have been given elsewhere. One example, however, will be cited, in order to give the flavour of these specific behaviour change tactics used in Buddhism. This account is from the *Dhammapada Commentary*.

> For a period in his life, King Pasenadi of the Kingdom of Kosala used to eat boiled rice by the bucketful, with equally large amounts of curries and sauces. One day after breakfast, feeling slothful as a result of overeating, he went to see the Buddha. Overcome with drowsiness he sat down on one side. 'What is the matter, King, did you not sleep well last night?' the Buddha asked. 'Oh no, Lord', the King replied, 'but I always have this problem after eating.' Then the Buddha said: 'King, overeating

causes problems. Anyone who lives indolently, eats large quantities of food, sleeps all the time, so that he rolls like a pig fed on grain, such a man is a fool because it is bound to lead to suffering.' The Buddha further said, 'King, one should observe moderation in eating, because that leads to comfort.' He then called the King's nephew, Prince Sudassana, and requested him to help. He was asked to memorise a verse containing advice on moderation in eating, and then gave him the following instructions: The prince was to watch the King whenever the latter had a meal. The moment the King was about to take the last handful of rice, the prince must stop him and recite the verse to remind him of the Buddha's advice. The King, thus distracted and reminded of the Buddha's advice, would then not eat that handful. Then, for the King's next meal, the prince should fetch only that much rice as he had been allowed to have the previous time, and so on. This programme went well, with the King co-operating enthusiastically in his training. In fact, if he had to be reminded by the prince of the Buddha's advice by reciting the verse at a meal, he would give away (not part of the Buddha's programme!) a thousand pieces of money in alms. The regime made the King lean and energetic again, as he began to eat a limited amount of food daily. Later he went and thanked the Buddha.

Summary

To recapitulate, then, the Buddhist theory and practice of behaviour change encompass different kinds of change. Firstly, there is the ideal of *arahant*hood – a state of human perfection that signifies a basic transformation of the person, thus entailing a radical change in behaviour. This state is achieved by a gradual process of development, of which both restraint in motor, verbal and cognitive behaviours and meditation exercises are significant components. Secondly, the importance of changing specific behaviours in day-to-day life, when and where required, is acknowledged. This is not only as a preliminary preparation for the cultivation of virtues necessary for the eventual development of the *arahant* state, but also because the Buddha recognised the value of healthy, dutiful and productive living in its own right. While prescriptive but reasoned teaching was one way of attempting to induce these changes, we have seen that there was also a wide array of specific behavioural techniques employed for this purpose. In addition, meditation of certain types was considered relevant in this domain, too, for achieving change in certain specific behaviours.

Buddhism and Psychological Therapy : Concluding Comments

In attempting to answer the question: 'What contribution can Buddhism make to psychological therapy?', both the above concepts of behaviour change have to be taken into account.

Personal development, *via* the means recommended for the attainment of the *arahant* state, has much potential value; perhaps not so much as therapy in the remedial sense, but – more importantly – as therapy in the prophylactic sense. Those who have reached a state of personal change of such a radical nature as to be able to react to the incessant flux of stimuli that assail them with calmness and equanimity, are clearly less vulnerable to the effects of stress and change around them. They are alert to their own experiences and responses, and here control over them. They are detached, compassionate and relaxed. Goleman has written of *arahant*hood as an ideal state of mental health, and of meditation – which is essential in the quest for this state – as providing a general pattern of stress-responsivity which is less likely to trigger the establishment of specific maladaptive responses. This is prophylactic therapy in the sense of primary prevention. It must be recognised, however, that the state of *arahant*hood is a difficult ideal to attain, and requires not only meditation but a life of great restraint, committed to the renunciation of worldly pleasures and attachments. In the context of today's world, very few if any would be willing or able to undertake such a path of total renunciation that necessarily negates much of what we normally take as essentials of life, including basic attachments, and aggression in self-defence. On the other hand, this does not preclude the feasibility of undertaking systematic meditative and self-development efforts in order to improve and enhance one's functioning, in terms of greater alertness, sharper acuity of perception of one's subjective states, a more relaxed attitude, and an enhanced ability to tolerate stress, frustration and loss. In other words, while *arahant*hood (which is a perfect state where the person is free from vulnerability to psychological afflictions, and is thus an ideal state of mental health) cannot be an immediate goal for a lay person, some of the self-management efforts that are recommended as essential in the quest for this state can still be of much use. They will contribute to developing a greater ability to face problems, worries and stresses of living and reduce the changes of these causing maladjustments and dysfunctions.

In the more directly remedial sense, the specific behavioural strategies found in Buddhism have clear relevance to current therapy. In fact, the efficacy of many of these techniques, in their present form as independently developed methods of clinical behaviour therapy, is well-documented. The existence of these techniques in the Buddhist literature two thousand years before the advent of modern behaviour therapy is not only a matter of historical interest; it also has clinical implications. If specific techniques found in the Buddhist tradition can be used in, or incorporated into, the psychological therapy offered to Buddhist client groups, it is likely that the therapeutic endeavour will on the whole be facilitated; it is not unreasonable to assume that the acceptance of therapy, and compliance with therapeutic instructions, will be greater. Therapy will not be seen by clients as an alien form of intervention, but received as something that fits well into their cultural tradition and belief system. The usefulness of offering therapy that matches the client in this way has already been commented on.

It will also be useful to subject to empirical investigation those specific behavioural techniques, including cognitive-behavioural ones, which up to now have no direct parallels in modern clinical practice. What is needed is the systematic testing of such techniques as interventions for the problems for which they are claimed to have been useful. This process of empirical testing may lead, hopefully, to the widening of the repertoire of behavioural and cognitive-behavioural therapies at the disposal of today's practitioners.

Before concluding this chapter, a final comment needs to be made. We have shown here, *inter alia*, the relevance of Buddhism to *behavioural* psychotherapy; this is in contrast to much of the previous literature and practice, which have highlighted its relevance to insight-oriented therapy. In fact, the behavioural aspects of the Buddhist theory and practice of behaviour change have been neglected until quite recently. It is clear, from our analysis, that Buddhism has much in common with the behavioural tradition of therapy, and has a contribution to make to this field.

15

BANKEI – SEVENTEENTH CENTURY JAPANESE SOCIAL WORKER?

People in the helping professions have a poor sense of their own history. Reading most contemporary texts, you might assume that helping people in any systematic way began with the Charity Organisation Society or the modern Welfare State. But priests have a long history of paid helping. For example, we have detailed records of Bankei Yotaku's 'casework' with ordinary people mainly from the year 1690.

Bankei was a Master in the Zen school of Buddhism. He was born in Japan in 1622 and died in 1693. At the core of Zen is a direct pointing into the heart through quiet sitting (*zazen*) and the eventual attainment of *satori* (awakening). Bankei achieved satori when he was only twenty-six.

The records kept by his attendant Itsuzan show him to be a man of great wisdom and humility. He spent most of his life outside the monasteries. He was very popular with ordinary people, who flocked to hear him speak. The problems they brought are very familiar to modern social work and counselling services. His replies owe little to Hollis or Biestek but allowing for three hundred years and eleven thousand miles, the differences are not vast.

Bankei stressed ordinary work as a means of meditation, establishing a harmony and balance in life. 'If your normal walking and standing, your sitting and reclining, are the work of a living Buddha, nothing remains to be done.' He had a direct experience of the unborn mind. 'For Bankei's Unborn is the root of all things and includes not only the sense-domain of our daily experience but the totality of all realities past, present and future and filling the cosmos.' This is close to Carl Jung's notion of the collective unconscious.

Bankei's teaching was based on his own suffering. The very young Bankei left school and returned home early to avoid a calligraphy class, which he disliked. His elder brother (the head of the family as his father was dead) ticked him off without effect. The brother told the ferryman not to take Bankei across the river between his home and school if he should return early. When Bankei was refused entry to the boat, he said 'The ground must continue under the water', strode right into the river and struggled to the other side. Later he decided to kill himself to avoid further conflict with his brother. He swallowed a mouthful of poisonous spiders and shut himself up in a small Buddhist shrine and waited for death. After a while he realised he was not going to die and went home.

Here are some extracts from Bankei's talks, which convey some sense of his understanding of human suffering, its causes and how they might be healed.

'At birth, each person receives a Buddha-mind from his parents. He is born with not a single other thing. Yet his illusions he produces by himself through his own one-sidedness. . .'

'In spite of the fact that you all came into this world with an unborn Buddha-mind and with nothing else, you are partial to yourselves, so you want to make things move in your own way. You lose your temper and become contentious. Then you think: 'I have not lost my temper. What that fellow says is so unreasonable that he has *made me* lose it. . .'

'. . .even a man who was until yesterday a great scoundrel, the object of everyone's contemptuous pointing and whispering, if from today on he recognises his past misdeeds and lives in accordance with the Buddha-mind, from this day forward he is a living Buddha.'

'No matter how many different thoughts arise, let them remain right where they are. Don's give thought even to what you may find delightful. You mustn't make your one mind into two. If your mind is always set like this, it won't think about what is good and what is not good. It won't think it should not think about such things, or that it should cease to think about them, and therefore thoughts of good and bad cannot help cease naturally. The same is true of displeasure and pleasure, which are both merely bred from your self-centredness.'

Here are some ideas familiar to modern social workers. 'He has *made me* lose my temper' shows an understanding of what just over 200 years later was to be described as 'splitting' and 'projection' – the psycho-analytic defence mechanisms. The idea of bringing different parts of the mind into unified consciousness is an essential element in the gestalt therapist's armoury.

Of especial interest are the accounts of Bankei at work. His teachings are based on the experiences of ordinary people. 'I never quote the words of the Buddhas or Patriarchs when I teach. I need only to examine directly the personal affairs of people themselves.' He would have failed any professional social work course on the grounds of inadequate theoretical and philosophical understanding.

A woman asked, 'I have a fear of thunder which is far out of the ordinary. Whenever I hear it, immediately I feel sick and suffer great anxiety. Please, tell me how I can somehow put an end to this fearfulness.'

Bankei said, 'When you were born you had no mind to fear things, only the unborn Buddha-mind. The illusion of fear for something is a figment of thought that was produced after you came into the world. Thunder benefits man by bringing rain into the world. It doesn't harm him. Your going afraid because you contend with the thunder is the work of that figment of thought; it doesn't come from outside yourself. When you hear the sound of thunder, trust single-mindedly in your own mind and Buddhahood.'

Many people who came to Bankei were concerned with dying and death. Often he saw that as an important and genuine gateway to experiencing real mental health and spirituality. The priest Jozen said, 'I'm greatly troubled about death. That's why I'm always coming here to see you. I don't think there could be anything of greater importance for a person.' Bankei responded, 'That mind is the fundamental source of Buddhist practice. If you come to think like that and do not lose your determination, you'll soon conform to the Way.'

During the long winter retreats many women travelled from all parts of Japan to see the great Zen Master. Some came grieving inconsolably having lost a parent or child. They believed that Bankei could help lessen their grief. Bankei talked quietly to them: 'The sorrow of a parent who loses his child, or of a child whose parent dies, is the same throughout the world. It is a matter involving the depth of the karma binding together the relation of parent and child and making us parents and children. It is in the nature of things for parents or child to grieve when death takes one from the other. Even so, for all grief and sorrow, the dead do not come back. In their ignorance, people lament continually with all their heart what cannot be undone. Was ever the return of a dead man achieved because of the zeal with which he was lamented? No.'

Some men came to see Bankei about their uncontrollable anger. Here he uses a family therapy technique – paradoxical imperative or something very like it. A monk addressed him: 'I was born with a short temper which is always flaring up. My Buddhist teacher has done his best to help me, but without success. I realise myself it is not good, and I try to correct it, but it is something I was born with so I have not been successful. . .'

Bankei responded: 'You have a very interesting inheritance. Is this short temper here now? If so, bring it out right this instant. I will cure it for you.' The monk said: 'I don't have a temper now. It appears suddenly when something irritates me.'

Bankei said: 'Then you weren't born with it. You precipitate it yourself on account of some chance cause. Such causes may arise, but still, where could the temper come from if you did not generate it. . .? Your parents gave you a

Buddha-mind when you were born, nothing else. From the time you were a tiny child you have watched and listened to people in their fits of ill temper and you have learned from them and imitated them, until irascibility has become a part of your own disposition too.' That is fairly close to a seventeenth century exposition of learning theory.

Bankei has like most Zen Masters a profound disrespect for the intellect as a source of real and fundamental human change. Here he pulls the rug from under the feet of this amateur psychologist. A layman said, 'Last year, when I was beset upon by confused and disordered thoughts and asked you how I could put an end to them, you told me to let the thoughts arise and cease without bothering about them. I accepted that. But later I found that it was almost impossible to do.' (It is just like Monday morning in Preston West Social Services office. The duty officer is confronted with 'I did what you told me on Friday and it didn't work. . .') Bankei despatches this client with 'It's difficult because you think there's a teaching that you should let thoughts arise and cease without bothering about them. You cannot get through personal turmoil through the imposition of yet another rule, even if you think it comes from me.'

A layman asked, 'When I get rid of a thought that comes into my mind, another appears right afterwards, and this continues on repeatedly. What can I do to overcome it?'

Bankei expounds on the same theme: 'Cutting off occurring thoughts is like washing blood off in blood. The original blood might be washed off, but you're still defiled by the blood you wash in. You can wash it as much as you like, the bloodstains won't go away. You don't know that your mind is originally unborn and undying, that it is free of illusion, and you think that thoughts really exist, so you revolve in the cycle of birth and death. You must realise that thoughts are temporary, changing appearances, and neither seize on them or hate them, just let them occur and cease of themselves. It's like the image reflected in a mirror. The mirror is clear and bright and reflects whatever is placed before it. But the image does not stay in the mirror. . .'

In the next story Bankei shows an understanding of what we would now call alcoholism – dependence on *sake* (rice wine). A layman said, 'I don't doubt that my thoughts are fundamentally without substance. Yet they keep popping endlessly into my head all the same, and I find it almost impossible to be the unborn, even for a short time.'

Bankei said, 'That's because although at the time you arrive in this world there's only your unborn Buddha-mind, as you grow up you become accustomed to seeing and hearing the manner in which ordinary people engage their minds, until, habituated to illusion over a long passage of time, the delusion of your own mind gets to be completely free and unrestrained, so if the mind trusts and affirms the unborn Buddha that it originally is, they will disappear.

It's like a man who loves *sake* but must abstain from it, because of bad health. The thought that he wants to drink still arise in his mind whenever he encounters a chance for a drink. Yet because he abstains from drinking it, he doesn't get ill, and he doesn't get drunk; he remains a non-drinker in spite of the thoughts of *sake* that arise in his mind, and ultimately he becomes a healthy man, cured of his illness. Illusory thoughts are like this. If you just let them arise and let them cease, and don't put them to work or feel any aversion to them, before you know it, they will disappear into the unborn mind.'

Bankei had little time for the formal trappings of religious practice – the temples, the incense, the long hours of austere meditation. He would have been impatient with social services bureaucracies. He grasped the heart of human suffering. In criticising his Buddhist teachers he got close to my feelings about modern social work. 'I am deeply grateful for all the teaching I have received from Buddhist teachers. It is not at all that I don't agree with what they say. Only somehow or other, the feeling I get is one of scratching at an itchy foot without taking off my shoe. They don't get directly to the itch. Their teaching does not strike home to my inmost being.'

Bankei not only expressed compassion, he *was* compassion. During one of his retreats, a student was caught stealing. Others reported it to Bankei and asked for his expulsion. Bankei ignored it. Later the student was caught stealing again and once more Bankei ignored the request for expulsion. The other students were angry and drew up a petition asking for the thief to be sent away or they would leave. He read the petition and called everyone before him. 'You are wise brothers. You know what is right and what is not right. You may go somewhere else to study if you wish, but this poor brother does not even know right from wrong. Who will teach him if I do not? I am going to keep him here even if all the rest of you leave.'

A torrent of tears cleaned the face of the brother who had stolen. All desire to steal had vanished.

16

MEDITATION : PSYCHOLOGY AND HUMAN EXPERIENCE

Scientific research on meditation represents a meeting of psychological methodologies from two quite distinct philosophical and theoretical backgrounds. Meditation may be described as the methodology of Eastern psychology in that it is a means to experiential knowledge of mind and self, whereas Western psychology has adopted the scientific approach to understanding, relying on procedures which are publicly observable and verifiable. The irony of this meeting is perhaps that we have learned little about meditation and more about our methods of enquiry.

In this chapter I shall describe the history of psychological research on meditation and briefly summarise the research results. Then taking a broader perspective on the history and type of research, it will be argued that our understanding of meditation has been as much restricted as developed by these endeavours. The results of in-depth interviews with long-term meditators in the West will be described and the implications for research discussed. It will be argued that existing methodologies have been allowed to determine our questions, rather than psychological theories (both Eastern and Western), and that this has further limited our appreciation of meditation.

Psychological and Medical Research on Meditation

Among the earliest studies on meditation were those carried out in the 1950s by Das and Gastaut, Bagchi and Wenger and

Kasamatsu and his colleagues. Their interest was primarily in physiological changes occurring during the practice of meditation, and they chose as subjects expert practitioners – yogis and Zen Buddhist monks. Indeed, Bagchi and Wenger transported sophisticated recording equipment around temples, monasteries and even into remote caves, to contact these meditators. The research showed unusual patterns of brain wave activity during meditation, especially during periods of 'samadhi' or ecstasy. While methodologically crude these early attempts to understand meditation were significant in their focus on accomplished practitioners of meditation rather than on novices.

Physiological Changes Associated with Meditation

Few studies were conducted in the West until the 1970s, though as early as 1960, Peter Fenwick, of the Institute of Psychiatry in London, reported at a conference in Marseilles on his studies of brain wave patterns during meditation. In 1970 Keith Wallace published details of physiological arousal levels during the practice of Transcendental Meditation (TM), creating a stir of interest among both psychologists and doctors. Wallace, Benson and Wilson argued that they had evidence of a fourth major state of consciousness (after waking, sleeping and dreaming) which was characterised by very low levels of physiological arousal. They reported significant and dramatic decreases in heart rate, respiration rate, oxygen consumption and skin conductance. However, with further studies and more careful research methods, the reliability of some of these results has been thrown into doubt. There is much doubt about whether, for example, heart rate and oxygen consumption decrease during meditation. Some reviewers see meditation has having no effects that distinguish it from simply sitting quietly, whereas others claim that meditation is important in bringing about a generalised reduction in many physiological system. What is clear is that studies of meditation have failed to establish that it is a fourth major state of consciousness – at least in physiological terms. The evidence suggests that there are decreases in arousal during meditation but these are not significantly different from decreases in arousal that can be achieved by other relaxation practices.

Little research has been carried out to assess the long-term physiological effects of the regular practice of meditation. In one six month longitudinal study, people learning and practising meditation showed significant decreases in spontaneous skin conductance responses (a measure correlated with anxiety) outside of meditation. This study also showed greater decreases in arousal during meditation as subjects practised regularly over the six-month period. Goleman and Schwartz, on the basis of their research, argue that experienced meditators show faster recovery from stressful experiences than do other people.

There has been much research interest in patterns of brain wave activity during meditation. The results of some studies suggest that meditation might simply be sleep by another name, while others suggest that meditation is a basis for creative ability and holistic growth. Overall the EEG research indicates that there is a pattern of lowered arousal during meditation and that it may be possible to differentiate meditation from other relaxing activities and altered states of consciousness by reference to patterns of EEG activity.

In summary, research on the physiological effects of meditation reveals decreases in arousal during the practice of meditation though it is not possible to isolate these as due specifically to the mechanics of meditation. Some remarkable changes in physiological functioning have been observed among expert practitioners of meditation but these have been single case studies rather than controlled studies of groups of meditators.

Meditation and Personality

It was shortly after the publication of Wallace and Benson's research that psychologists began to examine the effects of meditation practice upon behaviour and personality. Comparisons of meditators and non-meditators revealed the former to be less depressed, less anxious, less irritable, more self actualised and happier. Furthermore, long-term meditators were significantly less anxious than short-term mediators. Longitudinal studies have confirmed a causal relationship by showing decreases in anxiety and neuroticism over time among those learning and regularly practising meditation. Three characteristics of this research should be borne in mind. First, almost all the research focused on TM rather than other types of meditation. Second, only three studies examined changes in personality over a period greater than three weeks. Third, that a number of studies have shown that those attracted to TM are more anxious and neurotic than the general population and are therefore more likely than other groups to exhibit large changes on such measures.

Meditation as Therapy

Of the three major areas of meditation research – physiological changes, personality changes and therapy – therapy has been the least productive. Early interest was aroused by the possibility that meditation might be a useful treatment for drug addiction and irresponsible claims were made by researchers and meditators alike on the basis of inadequate research. While meditation has become increasingly popular as a therapy over the last 20 years, most studies evaluating its effectiveness have failed to overcome the methodological problems which dog research on psychotherapeutic outcomes. Benson and others in one of the more careful studies, compared self-hypnosis and meditation as treatments for anxiety. Thirty-two patients practised their techniques daily for eight weeks. Change in anxiety was determined by psychiatric assessment, self-assessment and physiological testing. Overall improvement occurred as a result of both interventions. The authors concluded that meditation is effective in the treatment of anxiety and is simple to use.

Woolfolk and others found meditation to be more effective than no treatment and equally effective as progressive relaxation in the treatment of insomnia over a six month period. The use of meditation in the treatment of hypertension has been carefully investigated. Most studies show only short-term decreases in blood pressure, dependent upon regular meditation practice, suggesting the importance of sustained practice for beneficial outcomes. There have been no large-scale and careful studies of the effectiveness of meditation as an adjunct in psychotherapy, though there are many interesting anecdotal reports of its use.

A major problem of interpretation of this research is that measurable effects may be created by the beliefs of meditators in the efficacy of meditation, that is, a kind of placebo effect, and that any technique, given similar credibility, would have similar effects. The use of the TM technique in investigations has compounded these problems since the teaching maximises attribution, placebo and expectancy effects. People learning TM are exposed to 'scientifically backed' claims for the benefits of the technique. The individual is also taken through a religious ceremony, asked to pay a sizeable sum of money and to participate in group discussions of the effects of meditation. Such a series of influences is likely to increase both expectations and subsequent belief in the efficacy of the technique. These beliefs are powerful factors in themselves in producing behaviour change. Such problems beset all research evaluating psychotherapeutic outcomes but are particularly difficult to overcome in this area.

So, some fifteen years of sustained research on meditation and over 1,000 published research articles reveals the following: (1) During meditation the body becomes a little quieter, a little stiller; (2) Regular practice of meditation is associated with decreases in anxiety though whether this is due specifically to meditation rather than simply sitting quietly is not known; (3) Meditation is as effective as selfhypnosis and progressive relaxation in the treatment of problems such as insomnia and anxiety, though regularly of practice seems important for effects to be sustained.

Why has meditation therefore been practised for thousands of years in a variety of cultures and religious and philosophical contexts if this is all that it accomplishes? Even a cursory knowledge of the practice of meditation in the East will testify that meditation is not viewed as simply a prophylactic for stress. The aim is usually to achieve a state and trait of consciousness which is an expression of fundamental religious beliefs about ways of being. Below I consider the reasons why psychologists have been so little concerned with these subjects and so much concerned with outcomes only marginally relevant in the traditional context of meditation.

The History of Meditation Research

When research into meditation first began in the late 1960s and early 1970s it was regarded by many psychologists and doctors as a rather esoteric and fringe area. Consequently those who pursued this interest may well have attempted to make their studies more respectable by using reputable methodologies which employed well-established dependent variable measures such as oxygen consumption, brain wave patterns, heart rate and even rectal temperature. To measure more complex changes in behaviour standardised questionnaire instruments such as the Eysenck Personality Inventory or Cattell's 16 PF or other paper and pencil tests were used. Many of the researchers were themselves 'new' meditators with an investment in discovering positive effects of meditation in their research. Conceptual analysis often sits uneasily with experiential knowledge and perhaps these researchers were eager to ease their own doubts about meditation. Hence, much of the research is on short-term easily demonstrated outcomes such as physiological parameters and gross personality change.

The research tended very much to follow a conventional 'medical model' approach. Those who participated as subjects in this research were viewed rather like patients with an illness, for which meditation was the hypothesised cure. Thus, measures of personality were taken before they began meditation practice and again after a short period of practice. 'Improvement' on these measures was then assessed. Meditation came to be seen as a kind of therapy for current maladies such as hypertension, drug abuse, insomnia, headache and even as an aid to memory and scholastic performance. Such concerns with short-term gains accruing from meditation practice have a peculiarly Western materialistic rather than Eastern orientation.

The emphasis on short rather than long-term effects of meditation is also apparent when we look at the studies examining physiological changes. Almost all have examined changes during meditation, rather than longer-term changes outside of meditation or changes during meditation but over a long period of practice. Personality is a term used to describe relatively stable and consistent patterns of behaviour, yet researchers in this area were looking for change over periods as short as three or four weeks. Similar criticisms apply to studies of meditation in therapy.

Perhaps part of the reason for this orientation is the marketing of TM in the West as a powerful and effective antidote to stress, with promises of a more effectively functioning nervous system and relief from psychosomatic disorders. Many scientists simply set out to evaluate the claims of the TM organisation rather than deriving their own hypotheses from theories or from examinations of the Western or Eastern psychological literatures. This is not of course a criticism of the method of marketing TM. The Maharishi's ability to combine the marketing of the West with the practical wisdom of the East has brought hundreds of thousands to the experience of meditation.

A final criticism of the research is its almost exclusive emphasis upon the experience of relatively novice practitioners and yet in the East meditation is a path to be followed for years in pursuit of such qualities as clarity, wisdom and compassion. This emphasis on novice practitioners is a pragmatic response to the perennial difficulty of finding sufficiently large numbers of volunteers for research studies. The experiments of psychologists are populated predominantly by undergraduate psychology students – a captive audience. Similarly, it has been because TM meditators are the easiest sample of meditators to contact that we find so few studies of long-term practitioners of techniques such as Zazen. The consequence of this bias has been a concern with short-term gross effects of meditation, compounded by the fact that many of those who take up TM lapse in their practice in the first three to six months and meditate only sporadically, if ever, thereafter. Estimates vary, but probably fewer than one third continue meditation with any regularly, that is, four or more sessions per week.

In conclusion, there is a clear need to go back to the basics and reconsider what we are examining and how we wish to understand it. It may, therefore, be instructive to talk with meditators about their experiences, their motivations and their practice to discover better the most appropriate directions for our research endeavours. Good longitudinal research is difficult to conduct in terms of time and effort but short-term studies have been of limited value. Study of meditation in its Eastern context suggests there is probably more to be gained by study of longer-term practitioners than relative novices. Finally, it is time that study of meditation went beyond TM to explore the experiences of those from a variety of meditative traditions.

The Lives of Meditators

The rest of this chapter reports preliminary results and observations from an ongoing longitudinal study of the lives and meditation 'career histories' of people who have been practising a variety of techniques over a period of at least three years. The study uses intensive interview data which are tape-recorded, transcribed and then content-analysed. The methodology is similar to case study analysis and is also based on the explicit recognition that the interviewer plays an important part in the process of the research through interaction with the interviewee.

The meditators who have participated in this research are drawn from a variety of backgrounds and are not intended to constitute a representative sample of long-term meditators. A number are psychologists, some are doctors, one is a teacher and others are social workers, engineers and unwaged women. The interviews are semi-structured around accounts of meditation career histories; experiences during meditation and changes in them over time; comparisons of the methods and experiences of different kinds of meditation; changes in daily life associated with the regular practice of meditation; significant experiences (good or bad) associated with meditation; the philosophical or religious context of the practice of meditation; whether a particular teacher or guru has been influential in the individual's meditation career; how meditation practice may have affected social relationships, relationship with self, attitudes to life and death; whether meditation is practised socially or in isolation; and why the individual practises meditation now.

Meditation Career Histories

Those who have participated in the research have meditation histories spanning, on average, thirteen and a half years, with a minimum of four years and a maximum of nineteen years. These figures do not always represent a period of sustained practice, since people sometimes stop meditating for a number of years or limit the frequency with which they practice. Nevertheless, in all of these cases, meditation practice has been sustained and regular for a period of at least the preceding two years and in most cases considerably longer. Descriptions of meditation career histories reveal a number of dimensions upon which each individual can be placed.

Intermittent versus Sustained

Some meditators do not practise with any long-term regularity. As one interviewee said: 'I find it hard to sustain any ongoing commitment for very long. It suits my style more to delve into things intensely and then come out and be relatively normal for a while.' Such a pattern seems particularly characteristic of the early years of meditation practice. Another said: 'I used to come back to doing it... if I was sitting at my desk and was very tired I would do it. It was a relaxing thing to do. If under stress I would do it for a little while and then stop. I felt better, but I didn't know if that was due to meditation or not.' Others are more sustained in their practice. Sarah, for example, has been practising meditation since she was 12 years old and for only one brief period in her 20s has she lapsed, though her meditation methods have varied considerably. There is some indication that periods of particular stress and turmoil may disrupt meditation practice. Barbara suspended her meditation practice during such a period: 'I feel there are great troughs in people's lives and meditation is just not always appropriate.'

Unimodal versus Multimodal

All of the meditators have practised more than one technique of meditation, with longer-term meditators being more likely to have experience of a rich mixture of methods. Julia began at the age of sixteen with breathing meditation at the end of her yoga practice and subsequently would focus on visual objects such as a candle, a stone or a flower. Later her meditations were on short pieces of reading material: 'I would read something like *'The Prophet'* and then think about it, sitting and contemplating it for about half an hour.' Richard learned TM while at University and since then has begun to learn Tai Chi. His sitting meditation now involves meditation on breathing. Anna however is determined to limit her experimenting: '. . . there is a time for exploration, but then at some point you have to take your trolley out of the spiritual supermarket and commit yourself to one discipline or you will never make progress.'

Group versus Solitary

Some come to meditation through groups such as the TM organisation and their careers are marked by moves from one such group to another. For others meditation is a solitary affair. Alistair taught himself a breathing meditation from a book and practised this for fifteen minutes daily. Since then he has attended a few lectures at the School of Meditation but disliked the 'bombastic and dogmatic teachings'. He still practises breathing meditation and also uses a mantra during his daily life, especially when walking. Recently he has met other meditators but is unsure about whether his involvement in a group will be sustained.

Social Support versus Social Conflict

Meditation can be solitary and even conflictual since some meditators are surrounded by family members and friends who regard their practice as odd or are even hostile to it. Richard's wife 'couldn't sit still to meditate and doesn't know what meditation is all about. She can't see any effect it has on me, and doesn't understand why I can't be natural, being a spontaneous person herself and far less self-conscious than I am.' For others there is much support and acceptance, especially if both partners in a relationship are meditators. Daniel says his family are 'very sympathetic and supportive and tolerant of individuality. I am very fortunate as they see meditation as simply something that I do. My wife goes to yoga classes although she herself is not a meditator. She practices yoga at home but it's not something I interfere with any more than she would interfere with my Tai Chi practice.'

Taught versus Acquired

This dimension overlaps to some extent with the Group-Solitary dimension and refers to whether the meditator has developed his or her own practice of meditation or whether formal teaching has been involved. For example, most of Jim's experience in his seventeen years of intermittent meditation practice has come from exposure to teachers. One of his first experiences was with TM and then he joined Bhagwan Shree Rajneesh's movement and learned a variety of different meditations. In visits to Zen Buddhist centres he learned Zazen, and has developed other meditation practices through similar contacts.

Effortful versus Gentle

Meditation can be a rigid discipline which involves finding time and practising with diligent efforts difficult meditations such as Zazen. Anna for instance feels the need for greater discipline and values the pressure of a group because '. . . one of the troubles about practising on your own is that I think

I'm doing it, but when I go to a weekend session, I see how slack I've become, so I'm evolving a more rigid context now.' Jim has approached all forms of meditation '. . . in a very gentle way. My attitude has been very non-grasping from the beginning.' He is much easier with himself being less concerned to maintain regular practice and adopting a more permissive attitude than Anna to the wanderings of his mind during meditation.

Spiritual versus Secular

For some meditators their practice is intrinsically part of a religious or spiritual life, while others reject religion. Jim falls somewhere in between. When asked whether he had any notion of a deity or spiritual entity, he replied: 'No certainly not. Because to have any such idea is to create a distinction between the creator and the created. And my image of God is not like a painting but like a dance. One is the whole thing. One is not controlling it. One is it. The dancer is the dance. Daniel is a Christian and attributes to meditation his 'very strong love for God, a much clearer more genuine love. I feel you can come to a much more direct experience in spiritual life through meditation, not just an academic thing you talk or think, but you actually feel something of the love which holds the world together.'

Advanced versus Novice

This dimension could be simply used to place the individual on the basis of years spent in regular meditation practice but this would imply that advancement comes from 'doing meditation time'. Alternatively one could rely on the individual to give an indication of their advancement at any one point in time (perhaps through standardised self-reports) but some will always describe themselves as 'spiritual babes' while others seem convinced by each new sensation that they are teetering on the brink of enlightenment. As interviewer I bring my prejudices to each situation, but I am sometimes left with a feeling that a person has some stillness, a clearer vision and may be a greater certainty than is usual. Perhaps this is too vague and subjective, for one can imagine other observers making different assessments. But then as Shapiro and Walsh argue: 'intellectual understanding in this area requires an experiential basis and what was incomprehensible at one stage may subsequently become understandable once an individual has sufficient experience of the meditation process.' These issues require much discussion and pose perhaps insurmountable problems for researchers. Nevertheless Eastern psychological theories challenge us to tackle them.

The value of the notion of the meditation career is in placing meditation in the context of the individual's life over time and broadens our attention to the longer timespan of experience rather than evaluating effects in terms of only short-term sensations and outcomes. The career dimensions also help to differentiate between meditators with different career patterns. The tendency to see meditators as a homogeneous group dominants the research literature and has obscured the large and real differences in people's experiences. As we shall see below, it is often the uniqueness of each individual's experience of meditation and not the commonality which seems most significant in the lives of meditators.

What is Meditation?

Most of those interviewed have practised a number of kinds of meditation and could identify some common essence across them. Sarah, who has been one of the most consistent over the years says it involves controlling the mind and always bringing it back to the object of meditation. This produces 'A feeling of centering and gathering your thoughts . . . just being really, being in that moment.' Jim says the most important component is 'the watching, the witnessing, being aware that you are aware, allowing the rise and fall of experience.' Jeffrey finds all meditation is a way of 'getting the mind to stop still. . . hooking the mind off its habitual concerns. The mantra gives the mind a job to do instead of fussing about with thought trains. The outcome is calmness and when the mind is calm, there it is.' For Julia meditation is 'any way of watching'.

Why Begin Meditating?

In 1975 I asked this question of eighty-three people who had learned TM and the vast majority were attracted by the possibility of gaining benefits such as relaxation, calmness and freedom from worry. Other reasons mentioned included desires for self-realisation and self-awareness. In the current series of interviews, Daniel, who has been practising for sixteen years on and off, but very regularly for the last five years says 'I had always been drawn towards it, because the study of one's mind seems to me crucially important. It was part of religious exploration.' For Julia the roots can be traced into childhood: – 'I can trace a religious interest right back. When I was about eight I built an altar in my room and had pictures up and sat in front of it. . .' Sarah too began meditation when quite young, at twelve and taught herself yoga and meditation from a book: 'The meditation would be things like imagining a candle flame or focusing on the feeling that no matter what went on around me, no one could take away the inner self. May be it's because I was an only child and I spent a lot of time alone.' Barbara had apparently more practical reasons for her initial interest: 'I had back problems and after reading a book on yoga began to practice both yoga and meditation.' For Alistair: 'It's a feeling of having an indirect experience of something you sense is there and want to reach. An intuition that there is something one is missing and meditation is a route to it.'

Jeffrey relates his interest to a spontaneous mystical experience in childhood in which 'I had the answer delivered to me on a plate and the whole of my intellectual and then practical interest in Zen Buddhism has been concerned with the recovery and understanding of the experience. It was a feeling of being totally overwhelmed in something utterly magnificent and extraordinary – an emotion filled with gratitude, wonder and incomprehension.'

Meditation Experience Over Time

The experience of meditation also appears to change in a consistent way over time. Meditators report greater ease of concentration and more stillness. Daniel, for example, is convinced that the experience of meditation changes over time: 'I think the awareness, the consciousness is clearer, so that if thoughts come up you remain aware of the breathing.'

Jeffrey too sees a change: 'It just gets easier to reach that state. When I began meditation using a technique of wallgazing it was very difficult, a real fight, not only the sitting but the thoughts of 'what am I doing here? Why am I sitting in a room with a Buddha image anyway? What is all this crap, this unscientific nonsense? Why not do something active like be a doctor? And then feeling imprisoned by the wall, wanting to punch it. But there is none of that now. I sit down and the practice will emerge fairly quickly, providing I'm not overtired, when it's better to sleep.'

The Effects of Meditation

The effects of meditation appear both subtle and pervasive in the lives of meditators. Anna tells how, when she initially began to meditate, she would read a Zen poem and explore the ideas in silent sitting which 'calmed me down and lifted me up'. Now she uses breathing meditation and Tibetan Buddhist meditations. The breathing meditation she finds 'does still the mind, does detach me from thought processes and reactions, from the events of everyday life. Meditation also deepens the feeling that it is OK to be me and that makes life a good deal more bearable.'

Daniel found that meditation helped him in the writing of his first book '. . . because by meditating just before I started writing I was able to clear the mind. . . and the writing became much more spontaneous.' Later there were more pervasive benefits: '. . . anger or fear or impatience. . . these are much less marked, less sharp. . . the smaller fears and anxieties that come along can be dealt with in a more detached way. By looking at them they go. . . looking as an observer, as a watcher, their impact is not so central. Julia too has found that her perspective has changed and she is less affected by 'these little things that niggle people. . . there seems to be so much more. I do think the world's a wonderful place and meditation enables you to see things as they really are in a still way.' Jeffrey finds his years of meditation practice have helped him to 'sustain an attitude and insight into life that the world just is and it's alright, and that the unseen is perfect in the fact of the ghastly social world of our times, and that even death doesn't matter.' But this experience of a broadening perspective is reported by even the relatively short-term meditators. Alistair, a relative novice, talks of feeling more relaxed and being less 'enmeshed in things that are not important'. This enables him 'to be more concerned with the moment'.

Jim talks at length about a change in the quality of his awareness and receptivity as a result of meditation practice. He experiences greater clarity: '. . . of thought, people and decisions and a sense of being very efficient when I want to be.' Along with this has come a subtle but profound change in his experience of himself 'in the sense that my experience and thought emerges as if there is a fountain or spring within me, the source of which is completely opaque to me. I experience myself as a conduit or a screen perhaps and less and less as a perpetrator. . . which has led to an attitude of interested passivity towards myself. . . a feeling of not being responsible for the generation of things. . . and a real interest and amazement and humour about myself and an attitude of friendliness and indulgence towards myself. . . my funny little ways. . . even the judgements I have about people.'

Perhaps such changes have adverse effects on those around. The interviewees do not think so. Jim feels more empathic: 'I can put my judgements on one side and see people and have a love for them and a compassion for them in the moment.' Jeffrey feels 'much less paranoid and more tolerant of other people, while Alistair sees himself becoming more intuitive in his relationships. Sarah's meditations on love, compassion and equality have had a 'very, very powerful effect in changing relationships and making me see other people in a different light. Without any sort of conscious change of mind, just by doing the compassion meditations regularly, you find yourself wanting to help other people and really caring just that little bit more. Before becoming a Buddhist, Sarah 'always felt that my happiness depended very much on other people and the relationships I had with them, and not so much on myself and the negativity I was carrying around. I had very much a feeling of self and other and other being different from self. Now I have an appreciation that self and other are not different. . .'

Changes in relationships and activities are experienced in work life too. Jeffrey cites his relationship with his boss. Tibetan Buddhism and the meditations have taught me to take on the problems of others instead of feeling angry. . . to see it from his point of view and think of him as a brother. That's part of the method of taking on the offending person as a loved relative. It doesn't work all the time. . . in emotional relationships it's much more difficult.' Anna is a doctor and meditation has proved useful for her work because '. . . the tools I have been given help me to face the pain and suffering in my job. . . I used to feel terribly helpless . . . Now I don't feel guilty that I can't solve the whole thing, and I can offer something human.'

But what all the meditators say is that changes occur gradually. Julia says that for this reason it is hard to say what effects meditation has, because 'it just creeps up on you over a long time, so it's a gentle accumulation of calmness, stillness, perspective and an ability to help others.'

Some meditators emphasise quite different effects from others, while some effects, such as a sense of perspective and ability to remain detached from minor upsets are shared by all. But another theme which emerges with constancy is the sense of 'being in this moment here and now'. Keith talks of moments of clarity which occur throughout the day and Barbara talks abstractly of '... it's not just you being more . . . you are changing, the 'beingness' also changes as you come to encompass it.' Matthew too talks of his self-awareness more continually becoming the object of his own awareness '. . . it intrudes in conversations, during sleep and even when I relax but it's taken a long time for these little twinkling experiences to become the object of my attention. . . but it is happening.'

Both Barbara and Julia describe how daily activities have become meditations and Jeffrey talks of even the washing-up sometimes feeling like an offering' . . . if you can stop and just gaze out of your eyes, with a sort of settling, the visual world just settles into itself. If you persist in it, it is almost as if the thinking mind stops and there is simply the acoustic, visual world just manifesting itself, which I find so powerful at times it almost brings me to tears – may be tears of relief. You can drop all the socially tiresome stuff and there is nature in itself.' Julia too talks of cutting off, being still and at one with everything: 'it allows you to be in touch with things as they really are. Things unfold in their own time, and it stops this awful Western way of wanting to make the world how you want it to be.'

The common elements in people's experience are striking but what also impresses is the variation depending upon the context of meditation practice. Thus, Tibetan Buddhism with its emphasis partly on relationships with others seems to evoke feelings of compassion and love. But even within a tradition each individual reports quite unique effects of meditation and the richness of their reports may be lost in attempts to group or summarise them. But there is a feeling too that the more meditators attempt to communicate their experiences in words, the more difficult it is for non-meditators to appreciate and understand the significance of the experience.

Significant Experiences Associated with Meditation

Of course, these people may simply be deluding themselves and rationalising hours of meditation sitting. If we asked those around them how their practice of meditation had changed them as people, we might find little corroboration. More objective research is needed. Such doubts perhaps prompted my expectations that many would report significant experiences, because I have the prejudice that some who are drawn to meditation techniques, unusual practices and traditions are perhaps sensation seeking. However, the majority of those I interview deny and significant experiences associated with meditation practice, telling only of gradual and subtle changes. Jeffrey says that he has come to develop an attitude of offering his life throughout the day and how with this has come a sense of gratitude and calmness 'which is far more enduring than that in enforced sitting. . .'

But Sarah is able to give an example, having recently returned from a two week solitary retreat. She found her meditations varied between being '. . . diabolical and those where I'd finish and somehow my whole environment was transformed. For a few moments quite genuinely seeing things in a different way. . . a very light quality about everything. . . very beautiful quality. It's the first time I've ever felt that meditation has transformed the way I look at things directly and not just intellectually.' And Daniel talks about driving in his car and '. . . becoming aware that I'm seeing something in a direct way instead of with concepts. . . seeing the world with the freshness of a child and a sort of blissful feeling.'

Why do they Meditate Now?

This was the most challenging questions for the meditators and its is the answers to this question which perhaps provide the clearest glimpse of what meditation means to these people. To Barbara 'It's my central belief, the heart of me. I feel I should honour that part of me. . all of it leads up to the purest expression of me.' Jim enjoys meditation because 'physically it feels good. . . interesting in terms of the insight that I get into myself and the more I can watch all this stuff going on and accept it, the more I can reveal myself to others.' Anna says '. . . it's the heart of life. . . It makes life whole. . . you can make it take in the whole day or eveybody you know or everything you have to do. . . it has that sense of pulling everything together, so it's a real centre.' Sarah meditates because it calms her down and she sees it as 'the only real hope to get rid of suffering by gaining complete control over the mind so that eventually your thoughts, feelings and actions are totally positive.' Julia finds it '. . . a way of being in touch with the universe.' One person emphasised the importance of the space that meditation provides her. She finds it a time of caring for herself, free from demands and needs and a time of being still and peacefully alone 'to allow her pure and perfect self to open more and more.'

Conclusions

By discussing with long-term practitioners their meditation career histories many questions of research interest arise and the paucity of the existing research literature in this area is underlined. Short-term investigations based on novice practitioners using only one kind of meditation fail to capture the deep significance of the place of meditation in people's lives. Research on meditation would seem to be best advanced by careful (though time-consuming and difficult) longitudinal studies, guided by careful theorising. The current research, as an example of a methodology, will be extended to include more long-term meditators and those already interviewed will be recontacted at intervals to chart the changes in their meditation and life experiences.

So many meditators talk of effects of meditation manifesting slowly, almost imperceptibly over time, confirming the importance of adopting longer term perspectives in research. And in this respect the notion of the career may be useful since it locates meditation in the context of the individual's life and helps us to recognise the need for studies of how it affects life attitudes and work experience. It becomes clear from this notion too that careers vary between individuals and simply grouping people on the basis of their shared interest in meditation may hide important differences. The interviews also suggest that research might explore the difference between types of meditation. And the aims of meditation should also be taken into consideration since interpretation of experience is likely to be much influenced by initial motivations. Finally for those who adhere to a religious or philosophical conceptual system, meditation has particular significance and functions which differ according to the system of belief and which have consequent impacts upon the interpretation of experience. These factors too much be considered in research.

The value of qualitative research at this time lies in helping to formulate new issues and problems which can be investigated systematically by more structured methodologies. It would, for example, be useful to explore the extent to which people become calmer outside of meditation and more detached from minor problems, and to compare different methods in this regard. Changes in patterns and quality of social interactions and in relationships among those who take up and sustain practices of meditation over a long period of time might also be plotted. Here too a focus on the context is important, since those from Buddhist traditions which emphasise compassion, love and equality may be more likely to experience changes in the quality of their social interactions. Reference to Eastern philosophies provides sophisticated conceptual frameworks to guide hypothesis development and within contemporary psychology many potentially useful theoretical orientations exist such as theories of self awareness, reversal theory, self concept theories, symbolic interactionism, theories of social judgement and attribution theory to name but a few.

The questions posed above entail difficulties of investigation, but over-simplifying questions may produce answers which only trivialise the experience. Research on meditation has often sampled the banal in meditators' experience and has illustrated the limitations of the nomothetic approach in areas of subtle and subjectively significant behaviour. The glimpse these interviews give us of the significance of meditation in people's lives illustrates how an ideographic approach at this stage provides unstructured but very rich data. Perhaps one of the consequences of this meeting of methodologies of East and West is that we are forced to turn back and examine psychological methodology more carefully. A repeated criticism of psychology is that the discipline focusses on phenomena which seem far removed from everyday subjective experience and that the most important experiences and events in people's lives are all too infrequently the subjects of inquiry. The study of meditation perhaps confirms both the need for a science of human behaviour to engage in exploration of people's most profound experiences and the importance of recognising the individuality of such experience and its place within the person's life.

17

THE NEW RELIGIONS AND PSYCHOTHERAPY : SIMILARITIES AND DIFFERENCES

Introduction

One of the most noticeable areas of individual growth and development over the past few decades, primarily amongst the affluent, young and self-aware, has been the search for self and for meaning in life, as witnessed by the growth of interest in two distinct fields of personal enquiry. These are the new religions (or at least new versions of old religions) often referred to as cults and psychotherapy. While the growth of psychotherapy has been on the whole welcomed by observers, the growth in the new religions has frequently been greeted with widespread alarm and condemnation. In this chapter, we shall look at this growth, and we will consider some of the differences and similarities of the two approaches. We will take as our primary focus of interest the new religions, rather than psychotherapy, as an adequate examination of the research concerning psychotherapy is outside the scope of a chapter such as this.

Unlike psychotherapy, cult phenomena have been the focus of much popular attention in recent years. The names of some of the new religions, such as the Moonies, the Orange people, Est, Hare Krishna, the Children of God and Scientology, have become household words. They have been widely commented upon by the media, politicians, the church, and also by various social scientists. They have particularly fascinated social scientists and psychotherapists, probably because of the striking psychological phenomena purportedly associated with them. These include the adoption of deviant life-styles, the rejection of the cult member's family, and extreme and occasional tragic occurrences such as the mass suicide/murder at Jonestown. They have also fascinated social scientists, we believe, because one of the grounds on which they have been criticised is their use of psychological techniques of persuasion and influence. These are techniques studied, even developed, by psychologists and psychotherapists, and which have been assembled, perhaps purposefully but often on an apparently ad hoc basis by the cult recruiters and trainers, and turned into avowedly irresistable procedures for 'brain-washing' their victims. The fascination for social scientists is quite possibly that of seeing their techniques actually at work; while the interest for therapists is perhaps alarm that major personal change is being effected in the recruits without the professional label of respectability which is usually accorded to psychotherapy, or the protection which is at least theoretically available to the consumers of a professional service.

The underlying theme of our chapter is that there is a need to re-examine at least some of the prevalent beliefs about the new religions, and in particular the popular evaluation of them hinted at above. We will do this by examining each of the grounds on which the new religions have conventionally been judged and criticised, and in each case look at whether these judgements are in fact justified and can be sustained, especially in the light of their similarity in processes and outcomes to the more 'respectable' procedures used in psychotherapy. In addition, we shall examine the issue of whether in fact many of these new religions actually function as religions, as whether in reality they act as a form of psychotherapy for many of their followers.

Let us say at the outset that we are *not* arguing that the new religions are 'a good thing' because they may resemble psychotherapies. We will be trying to show that the verdict of 'guilty' that has so far been passed on the cults is, we believe, based on an inadequate consideration of the evidence. However, we don't think that that makes the new religions 'not guilty'. Rather, we think that *some* of them are profoundly 'guilty,' and are destructive towards their members, but that it is not possible to understand which ones, why, or how to respond and deal with them and their victims until our own thinking about them has been clarified. That is what we shall be trying to do in this chapter, by examining them alongside and in comparison with psychotherapy. Similarly, in considering this parallel between the two types of activity, we are not making a claim that psychotherapy is necessarily a 'good' thing in itself, either. Psychotherapy, like the cult groups, may help some people in some ways at sometimes during their lives. We intend to argue that the way in which the new religions are effective relates quite closely to the ways that psychotherapy is effective, and it may well be the case that for at least some individuals, involvement in a new religion is no more harmful than involvement in perhaps a rather prolonged and intensive form of psychotherapy.

In addition, we do not wish to deny that there are some very big and significant differences between the two types of practice. For example, most therapy patients do not give away many of their material possessions to the therapist (although they may in some cases pay out considerable sums of money in fees). Nor do they tend to change their names or country of residence in order to be near the therapist, as cult members sometimes do. The families of therapy patients tend not to get so upset about the changes that occur as do those of cult members (although the changes that may take place in therapy do sometimes cause family problems). However, the order of magnitude of involvement is clearly different, as is the extent and nature of the reaction to those changes.

Definitions

Before proceeding further, we need to define exactly what we mean by 'the new religions', or cults. In Webster's 1966 Third New International Dictionary, there are three definitions of the word 'cult': (1) A system for the cure of disease based on the dogma, tenets or principles set forth by its promulgator to the exclusion of scientific experience or demonstration; (2) great or excessive dedication to some person, idea or organisation; and (3) a religion or mystic regarded as mysterious or unorthodox. Each of these definitions implies that members of what we call cults typically: (1) adhere to a consensual belief system which is deviant in at least some particular with respect to the dominant cultural context; (2) sustain a high level of within-group cohesiveness, and reject participation in the majority culture; (3) are strongly influenced by group behavioural norms (that is, are conformist); (4) impute charismatic (or divine) power to the group or its leadership; and (5) are deviant with respect to the dominant religion.

Obviously, all-encompassing definitions such as the above are inadequate: for example, we may not be justified in treating all of the groups as equivalent, and as having similarly characteristic ways of behaving. (The same point must also be made about the psychotherapies.) Nevertheless, these definitions all point towards a key aspect of groups which are labelled as 'cults': they reject the values and norms of the popular culture in favour of their own unorthodox views. It is the suggestion of some writers that this fact provides the key to understanding the common response to the cults: their unorthodoxy threatens the power and control of the orthodox religions and therapies, which must reject the value of the new religions largely because they are dangerous competitors and rivals. Indeed, it is interesting to note that some of the main sources of condemnation have been therapists as well as churchmen. It therefore seems to us that in many ways new religions and therapies are 'competing' for the same groups of people: the young, affluent and self-questioning.

In order to examine the argument that the processes by which the cult groups function in many ways parallel those by which psychotherapists function, we shall examine a number of aspects of the new religions: their mode of operation; their content; their recruits and their consequences. In each case, we shall look at the ways in which the new religions have been castigated, to see whether the objections to them are in fact reasonable or not.

Processes Used by the New Religions

A simple-minded comparison between the processes and methods employed by psychotherapists, and those employed by the new religions, might suggest that the one is carried out on a voluntary basis, in the interests of the patient, whereas the other is carried out using techniques of brainwashing, and is not in the interests of the cult member. It is not hard to find accusations of this kind, by sampling typical newspaper stories. For example: 'How love-bombed Mrs. Olsen needed to be deprogrammed' (from The Guardian, 9th November, 1983); 'Cult Drove My Kevin to the Grave' (from Bradford Telegraph & Argus, 4th December, 1984); 'German Industrialist Abandons all for Christ' (The Guardian, 21st February, 1985); and perhaps the most famous headlines of all: 'The Church that breaks up families' and 'They took away my son and raped his mind' (from the Daily Mail, 29th May, 1978). The Times (1st April, 1981) reporting on the outcome of the libel case brought by the Moonies against the Daily Mail as a result of these headlines and the articles that accompanied them, used the following headline: 'Cult's "love bomb" that was better than a gun'; and The Guardian, in rather more measured terms, reported that: 'Jury agree that Moonies cult is brainwashing' (Guardian, 1st April, 1981).

The accusation of brainwashing is clearly a key one, and one which needs examination in more detail. The term 'Brainwashing' was first used by an American Journalist, Edward Hunter, as a translation of the Chinese colloqualism 'Hsi Nao', which literally means 'Wash Brain'. It was used to describe the processed by which prisoners of war in Korea and elsewhere were assumed to have been persuaded to become sympathetic to the views of their captors. The popular image of brainwashing was that it was an enormously successful operation, by which innocent soldiers were turned into mindless communist sympathisers. It is used nowadays to explain the way in which recruits are said to be coerced into rejecting family and friends, and become devoid of individual personality or personal responsibility.

Now, if the new religions can be said to be brainwashing their recruits, most people would probably say that they cannot be understood to be acting in the best interests of their members. Instead, they must be acting in the interests of the cult, which is presumably destructive of individual personality. Brainwashing is assumed to be an all-powerful technique, which is somehow achieved by imposing the will of the evil collective or ideology on to the unsuspecting and unwilling victim.

An important component of this view of the process is that it is irresistible. Yet evidence shows that this is far from being the case. For example, in Korea, of the 7190 American prisoners who were taken and subjected to 'brainwashing', only twenty-one remained in Korea after the war, and the majority of these returned after eighteen months or so. Likewise of the British, out of 980 prisoners of war, only one remained behind in Korea. So even if the charge of brainwashing were to be sustained, this does not mean that the new religions thereby possess an irresistible means of conversion. So how in fact do the cults fare as 'brainwashers'?

The answer is, not very well. But an immediate qualification which has to be made is that it is obviously difficult to generalise about all of the new religions together, so we shall therefore consider those new religions at whom the charge of brainwashing has been most frequently levelled. The Unification Church (the Moonies) are perhaps the clearest case to consider, for as we have seen, the British courts have upheld the claim made by the Daily Mail that the Unification Church employs brainwashing techniques in its recruitment activities. Barker reported that of every 100 people who attended an introductory weekend workshop, only thirteen affiliated in some way to the Church, and only eight of these joined as full-time members. Less than four people remained as members after two years. If we examine figures presented by the Unification Church itself a similar picture emerges. At the end of August 1981, it was announced that the Moonies' 300 strong team of 'specially-trained' missionaries was leaving Britain. They claimed that during their three-years stay in Britain they had converted 2000 people (Guardian, 26th August, 1981), a success rate of 2.2 convertees per recruiter per year. These figures seem to compare rather unfavourably with those achieved by the average insurance salesman. Thus, the impression of an all-powerful recruitment technique seems to fade, and to be replaced with a more realistic image of a social movement using conventional (if somewhat unsuccessful) techniques of persuasion to recruit people to its view of the world, and to membership of the group.

Of course, one of the objections to the new religions is not only the way in which they actively encourage the process of conversion, but the way that they even more actively discourage members from seeking disconfirming evidence for the group's theology or values. Most observers confirm that the process of recruitment to one of the new religions involves a intense, emotionally charged period during which time the person's existing ties with the world are challenged, and replaced by new structures, which are more in line with the beliefs held by the religious group. But it should also be noted that many members of the cults, including members of the Unification Church live, not in sealed, isolated and restricted communities but as ordinary members of society. We should also note that an examination of the experience of patients in psychotherapy suggests that parallels exist between the process of conversion to one of the new religions on the one hand, and successfully engaging in psychotherapy on the other. If individuals seek psychotherapy, they are usually expressing some form of discontent with an existing way of behaving and thinking. Hence, the first job of any competent therapist is to help patients let go of some of their troublesome, although safe, current ways of behaving. This has to be done by challenging the patient's current understanding of themselves and the world, and encouraging the patient to develop new ways of being in the world. The only way that patients can possibly allow this to happen is if they trust the therapist, and are prepared, at least for a while, to suspend their commitment to current ways of acting and thinking. The therapist then has to encourage patients to experiment with new and hopefully more effective ways of behaving: ways which tend to be informed by the therapist's own view of the world, as well as the therapist's professional theories about what is desirable or 'mature' behaviour. Understood in this way, the role of the therapist is that of an encourager and persuader, who attempts to help the patient to see things more like a mature person (such as the therapist) sees them. In effect, the therapist persuades the patient to become more like the therapist.

According to Frank, the process of psychotherapy is simply a modern version of healing which has been happening throughout the centuries, in all human societies. Frank identifies six key features of healing, which he believes bring about change, largely through the process of persuasion. These features include the presence of socially sanctioned healers who have a rationale or myth to explain their actions; a willingness on the part of the 'patient' to submit to the healer's wisdom; and a set of rituals which mark the 'patient's' acceptance of his or her role. It seems that at least some of these features are also present during recruitment to the new religions. In addition, recent work on the effectiveness of psychotherapy has suggested that the way in which it works is primarily through the operation of non-specific factors, which include features of the therapeutic relationship such as hope, faith, the opportunity to express feelings, and so on. Such components may also be said to be present at least in the conversion phases of recruitment to cult groups.

As we have seen, during psychotherapy patients submit to a process by which their existing way of making sense of the world is systematically dismantled, so that a new, more effective way of functioning can be assembled. Patients entrust themselves to the therapist, and allow the therapist to learn all sorts of personal and intimate information. There is ample evidence that therapists have considerable influence over their patients, and, despite protestations to the contrary, systematically persuade their patients to change in a variety of ways. Yet the new religions are castigated when they appear to do the very same thing.

Although a reasonably similar change process can be observed in individual therapy and cult involvement, the parallels between the operation of the new religions and psychotherapy can be most clearly seen in group therapy. Group therapy is a process by which the therapist uses the power of group dynamics (such as conformity pressures, group loyalty, modelling and so on) to reinforce change in the individual. Many group leaders consciously make use of the very human tendency on the part of group members to want to belong and to receive approval from others, in order to establish a group norm of sharing and supporting which is part of the process of therapeutic change. A number of researchers have pointed out that a key feature of effective therapy groups is cohesion. Such facts have not passed unnoticed by the cult recruiters, who also use group loyalty, conformity pressure, and plenty of positive reinforcement for conforming to group norms, both to recruit and maintain membership.

Content of the New Religions

The next way in which the new religions are often attacked is on the basis that they have bizarre, inhuman beliefs, which are unreasonable and factually inaccurate. Although it is difficult to make general statements about the belief structures of the new religions, one thing is fairly clear. Many if not most critics do not actually know what many of the cult religions believe, so that the majority of judgements are based on prejudice rather than knowledge. But given particular content, how are judgements to be made? For example, the Moonies believe that God intended Adam and Eve to marry and have perfect children, thereby establishing the Kingdom of Heaven on Earth. The devil intervened, in the shape of the snake and seduced Eve. Eve passed her impurity on to Adam, bringing about the Fall. But how do we judge whether this is good or bad? It is our opinion that this is largely a matter of values and social consensus, not of fact.

Furthermore, such beliefs which may seem peculiar taken out of context, can easily appear reasonable or even logical, within the appropriate context. It is perhaps important here to compare such a belief with other, more conventional beliefs. For example, the traditional Christian belief holds as a sacred truth that the Son of God was born of a Virgin, performed a number of miracles, was crucified and was clinically dead for three days, after which He was resurrected from the dead, and ascended to Heaven. In His name, believers regularly eat and drink symbolic representations of His blood and body. The point of this is simply to demonstrate how bizarre common beliefs may appear when taken out of context, and without the mythic richness which is given by a community which understands the symbolic truths represented in the simple story. The same doubtless applies to many of the truths espoused by some of the new religions, although most critics do not take the time to enquire.

However, there are beliefs and practices espoused by some of the cults about which we do feel able to make judgements, and which appear to us to be morally bankrupt: for example, the belief that the ends justify the means. This belief underlies and justifies strategic behaviour, such as lying to new recruits, manipulating and deceiving members of the public and so on. In no way do we want to be understood as condoning such behaviour. But we also believes that in acting in this way, members of the new religions are not behaving differently from members of many other groups who also believe that the end justifies the means. For example, many groups believe in the use of violent revolution, or in censorship during warfare, because these acts are said to be in the long-term interests of the group. Indeed, the Christian religion is a good example. In the name of Christ, believers have tortured and murdered thousands of non-believers throughout history; here too the ends were said to justify the means. Another example might be the involuntary incarceration of some patients in mental hospitals, for treatment against their will, which is assumed to be in their long-term interests.

It is most important to reiterate here that we do not wish to suggest that the beliefs or practices of any particular cult are morally acceptable to us, or in particular that we in any way support Moonie beliefs and practices. However, we do want to argue that if we condemn the Unification Church, the Scientologists, or any other sect on the basis that their beliefs are irrational and inhuman, or that their actions are unethical and intolerant, then we must also apply these self-same standards to our own beliefs and actions. And if we apply the same standards to other areas of life we find that some of our most respected institutions may be equally 'guilty', as are some of our therapeutic practices.

Characteristics of Those Joining the New Religions

One of the most frequently heard accusations made of the new religions is that they tend to attract people who are in need of psychological help, and those who are inadequate or even psychologically disturbed. A number of researchers have looked at the characteristics of recruits to the new religions, and have reported evidence which seems to confirm this. For example, whilst it appears that most recruits come from middle class families, and may well have above average educational level, a common antecedent of those joining is some sort of trouble in the family. Another background variable seems to be excessive anxiety about the approach of adulthood. Typically, recruits are at a stage of life in which they are open and receptive to new ideas and experiences. The stereotyped picture of the rather lost-looking young person *en route* for nowhere in particular and being picked up by recruiters at the railway station, is not without some basis in reality. Levine reports that cults do tend to attract individuals who are in some psychological pain before joining, and Etemad has described cult recruits as 'depressed, inadequate, or borderline anti-social youths'. According to

Galanter 'their preoccupations with purpose and destiny are closely associated to a dissatisfaction with interpersonal relations, leading to loneliness and a sense of alienation.' A marked degree of use of illegal drugs prior to recruitment has been noted by other researchers.

Although most researchers are agreed on the finding that many recruits are looking for some deeper meaning and purpose in their lives, they dispute whether there are more than the average number of deeply disturbed individuals amongst their ranks. Some researchers have failed to find evidence of an excess of serious mental disturbance amongst members of the new religions, and point out that like any population, there are bound to be some with psychiatric disorders. On the other hand, others suggest that there does seem to be some evidence of a greater than normal level of psychopathology amongst recruits: for example, several report a higher than average number of cult members with some pre-existing degree of psychiatric disorder.

Of course, there are considerable methodological problems with retrospective reports, in that people may obviously colour their accounts according to the particular view that they currently wish to espouse. Nevertheless, it does seem likely that the new religions do attract a substantial number of people who are in some psychological distress and yet who also have some degree of willingness to change. Prior to joining the group, such people seem to be dissatisfied with their personal circumstances, and to be ready to do something about them. Given the nature and extent of the personal and social changes involved, it would be surprising if circumstances and motivations such as these did not exist amongst recruits. As such, the new religions obviously appeal to people similar to those who are attracted to psychotherapy, and want to change something about themselves. Interestingly, some writers have noted an increasing tendency for some individuals to try out both sources of help, and to progress, possibly rather indiscriminately, through a number of different therapies and religious groups until they find one which suits them. But it is hard to understand how the new religions should be held responsible for the alienation and human confusion that they are seeking to alleviate, any more than doctors should be held responsible for the illnesses that they are seeking to cure.

Consequences of Joining one of the New Religions

If as suggested above, the impetus for seeking either psychological help or membership of a religious group is reasonably similar, so the outcome of both types of involvement are to some extent parallel. In brief, although some individuals do appear to be harmed by the experience, the majority appear either to gain psychologically from their involvement, or to be relatively unaffected. Galanter points out that in 1920, William James wrote of religious conversion as a process whereby a person who is confused, inferior and unhappy, becomes certain, superior and happy. The consequences of joining a cult religion can be similar to those of conversion to any other belief system: increased certainty, confidence and contentment.

Of course, as in the psychotherapies, the outcome is likely to be different for different people: for the lost and lonely the new religions may provide a structure of meaning and a community of like-minded people; while for the deeply disturbed, they may provide a form of asylum. Levine concludes from a clinical examination of research into cult group membership that 'Cults do significantly reduce symptoms of anxiety, depression, (and) confusion in members who experience these.' She also points out that 'Cults do at times serve as a haven, and even a therapeutic milieu for members with serious psychiatric behavioural disorders.'

In addition, Levin and Zegans report the case of a schizophrenic youth who was profoundly helped by his unconventional religious beliefs, and conclude that: 'Many of the members of the new religions are seeking what has always been available to the shaman, a structure of meaning into which his own idiosyncratic experiences can be fitted, a tradition which guides and shapes otherwise bewildering and frightening psychological states. For these participants in the new religions, cults sustain the legitimacy of their experiences and provide a viewpoint from which they can be interpreted.'

On the other hand, it is without doubt true the *some* individuals are harmed by cult group membership. Levine concludes that 'Cults do contribute to the appearance of emotional problems in a significant number of ex-cultists,' and Singer believes that ex-cult members are likely to suffer from depression, severe passivity, indecisiveness and loneliness, in addition to considerable fear of the cult. Conway and Seigelman talk of the dangers of 'snapping' into a robot-like state, in which the individual is unable to think or act for themselves. However, Galanter points out that these negative reactions are much more common amongst those who had been forcefully 'de-programmed' than those who chose to leave of their own accord.

But the same is also true of some psychotherapies. Recent research on the outcome of psychotherapy suggests that while many patients will benefit from therapy, a small proportion actually appear to be harmed by the process. In addition, Lieberman, Yalom and Miles point out that some psychotherapy groups produce 'casualties': individual who leave their therapy much worse than when they initially sought help; while Llewelyn provides details of some of the unethical practices which sometimes occur in psychotherapy, particularly of a sexual nature, and which can cause longlasting and serious problems for therapy patients.

Even more seriously, some psychotherapy groups can themselves become rather like cults, and while purporting to be devoted to increasing an individual's psychological health, they can in fact do the opposite. Temerlin and Temerlin describe how a number of professional therapists have abused their professional position to set up groups which encourage obedience and adoration by the 'patients'; likewise, Hochman provides details of some of the coercive and destructive activities which have been labelled 'therapeutic' by a number of therapists who work well out of the way of professional scrutiny and study.

Conclusions and Implications

The above analysis of the process, content and outcome of involvement in the new religions, points to the fact that a judgement is being brought against them which is based not so much on objective, psychological evidence, as on a criticism of the beliefs and values of these religions. Yet it appears that many commentators are saying that cults should be condemned and restricted, *not* because they disagree with what the cults believe, but because of the consequences which they imply follow from the way in which the cults present their beliefs. However, as we have shown, it is not clear that this evaluation is based on a rational analysis of any objective evidence characterising the cult phenomenon: recruitment, content or consequences.

One clue to what in fact could be the basis of this criticism is given precisely by the fact that no distinctions are made between the different new religions. It is precisely what they have in common that is the basis of criticism. And what they have in common is an opposition to the *status quo:* both the *status quo* in contemporary religion, and in the psychotherapeutic establishment. Hence, one way of understanding the pervasive negative evaluation of the new religions is to see it as self-interest on the part of commentators and even researchers who see the cults as threatening because they represent 'unfair' competition. An additional clue is given when we compare the evidence and interpretations offered by different kinds of researchers. Broadly speaking, the most 'hostile' research has been presented by researchers working within psychiatry and psychotherapy, less hostile research has been presented by psychologically-orientated researchers, and the least hostile, most temperate analysis have been those produced by sociologically-influenced researchers. But as we noted at the beginning of the chapter, the new religions and psychotherapy are competing for exactly the same client group; the young, the affluent, and the self-aware. Could this hostility then be related to simple social and economic competition, a pressure not influencing the judgements of psychologically and sociologically orientated researchers, who are thereby able to adopt a more truely disinterested perspective? In a revealing article in the 'house-journal' of the American medical profession, Clark argues:

> . . . [the physician] may not immediately appreciate the degree to which the medical profession as a whole is under attack by these organisations. For one thing almost all embrace magic in many forms, including faith healing, and in their general rejection of their surrounding culture discard scientific linear thinking: thus, they reject modern medicine and consider physicians as enemies. In practice even those cults which occasionally use medical facilities are extremely reluctant to seek this help or *to pay their bills.* (our emphasis)

The response of the leaders of the established religions can also be understood as, in part at least, a reaction to the challenge posed by the new religions to their moral and social authority. The importance of the challenge posed in terms of simple competition for converts, and the economic power that these converts represent, should also not be underestimated. By extension, the response of opinion leaders within politics, the law, the media, etc. should also be seen in the light of the need to defend the existing social order. Viewed on this way, reactions to the new religions can be seen as another example of the 'moral panics' described by Cohen and characterised by outrage and over-reaction (as well as confusion). In the perspective of history and social change, many of today's most well-respected religions, for instance the Society of Friends (Quakers), the Mormons and even the Moral Re-armament movement within the Church of England, were subjected to, and have survived similar attacks.

However, as we have hinted throughout this chapter, our *personal* evaluation of the new religions is a generally negative one, and we feel that we should state the criteria against which we have formulated our judgement. These are: (1) Do we agree with, and approve of the teachings of that particular cult? (2) Do we believe the teachings of that particular cult to be true and correct? (3) Do we believe that the cult, and its agents, act morally in their dealings with its own members, and with non-cult members (for instance, does it lie, cheat and deceive)? Against these criteria, there are few cults which we personally find attractive. However, the essential point to be made is that these are non-psychological criteria and judgements. They are criteria which concern personal values, beliefs and attitudes, and we accept that our evaluations are in this way subjective and value-laden. What we hope we have demonstrated is that this is the only legitimate basis on which such evaluations can be made.

The attempt to invoke psychological perspectives, theories and evidence as the basis for, and as the legitimation of, criticism of new religions also has a number of implications for psychology (and for the other social sciences). The first of these is that it is important that those involved in any debate of this kind should make explicit the ethical/value issues that are involved, and if this is not done willingly, it should be one of the first issues addressed by any psychologist invited to comment on, or wanting to take part in the debate. The second implication is that, if we offer criticisms, based on psychological analysis, of the worth of particular phenomena, we should also be prepared to consider the ethical issues raised by our own technologies, and we should be prepare to judge ourselves by the same standards. This would force us to spell out, for instance, in the areas of individual and group psychotherapy, the nature of, and the relation between process, content and outcome in terms of their ethical consequences. At the present time the ethical acceptability of these practices appears to be one of the 'taken-for-granteds' of the psychotherapeutic enterprise. An additional implication is that, whilst the citing of psychology and psychologists in controversies over the new religions is in many ways a positive trend, indicating the acceptance of the psychological perspective as an important and useful one, it also has its dangers. These are the readiness with which acceptable standards of evidence and analysis can be abandoned in 'the rush to judgement', and the related way in which the professional and critical role of the psychologist can be so easily misappropriated.

We would like to end on a positive note, which we have found useful in our evaluation of the claims of both the supporters of the new religions, and of various therapeutic theories. The following quotation was used by Vaughan in her discussion of the new religious movements, and we have found it as apposite as she did. The words are those of Buddha, in the Kalamas Sutra, and in our view, should represent the attitude of the careful and scientifically minded observer of the new religions.

> Do not believe in what you have heard; do not believe intraditions because they have been handed down for many generations; do not believe in anything because it is rumoured and spoken of by many; do not believe in anything merely because the written statement of some old sage is produced; do not believe conjectures; do not believe merely in the authority of your teachers and elders. After observation and analysis, when it agrees with reason and is conducive to the good and benefit of one and all, then accept it and live up to it.

18

PSYCHOTHERAPY AND TECHNIQUES OF TRANSFORMATION

PART I

Religion as Psychology

'Does therapy lead to spiritual life?' asks Frans Bakker, an adept of Da Free John, and many have answered in the negative. But if participants in a fair number of new religious movements are to be taken seriously, psychotherapeutic techniques *do* have an important role to play in the spiritual quest. Indeed, if this testimony is counted as evidence, those who see therapy as incompatible with spirituality have got it wrong. For example, *est,* as Werner Erhard's initiatory seminar used to be called, draws techniques from the Western psychological tradition which are put to the service of 'enlightenment'. The flourishing nature of Erhard's organisation and the testimonies of participants appear to belie the incompatibility thesis.

Positive assessments of the role of psychotherapy within spiritual contexts are backed up in the final sections of this chapter. One argument is that 'secular' psychotherapies can work on the 'ego' in ways which almost demand their employment in spiritual paths. However, some of our discussion of what it is about psychotherapy that has allowed it to be used as a technique of transformation should also please the advocates of incompatability. But because spiritual matters lie beyond the province of academic proof (they fall outside the scope of logic and empirical assessment) we limit ourselves to presenting different interpretations as alternatives. There are a number of ways of understanding the relationship between psychological techniques and spiritual realisation. We leave it to those who have first hand experience, or second hand prejudices, to make the choice they desire.

Incompatability

Psychotherapy, many would argue, is scientifically informed. The medical approach is often to the forefront. Scientifically grounded methods are employed to enable people to change themselves. The goal is to acquire self development, or rather self normalisation, in a fashion which accords with what is scientifically (and socially) possible. With this frame of reference, religion or spirituality is the enemy. It is positively harmful to rely on religious 'mumbo jumbo' in a desperate effort to find salvation. Crutches have to be knocked away. What matters is strengthening the ego, many still agreeing with Freud's view that 'where there was id, there shall ego be.' Surrender to father figures or to oceanic spiritual experience can only be damaging. Such reliance is bound to threaten what is all important, namely scientifically demonstrated means of obtaining socially defined ego identities.

Therapists such as Freud argue the incompatability thesis from the side of science and society. However some advocates of the spiritual path, now treating the ego as the enemy, argue to the same end. Bhagwan Shree Rajneesh, for example, hates conventional psychotherapy. Cultivation of the ego is intrinsically damaging:

> Western psychology still thinks in terms of a healthy ego. But ego can never be healthy. It's a contradiction in terms. Ego, as such, is ill.

Cultivation of the ego attaches people ever more strongly to the limitations of the human sphere. Lying 'beyond' the ego, realisation of the freedom and natural virtues of the spiritual domain is ruled out of court. The spiritual domain can only be realised when people go to a master, someone who works to an end which stands in stark contrast to that held by the psychotherapist. For, continues Bhagwan, a master –

> doesn't help you to attain a stronger ego. He makes you feel that the ego you have is already too much. Drop it! Let it go!

Only then can you be 'whole and flowing'.

How on earth can psychotherapies, aiming to handle fear, guilt, anger and the like by developing a functional ego structure, be of any use to the spiritual enterprise? It certainly looks as though ego identification simply enhances the very thing which cuts us off from spiritual experience. It certainly looks as though going *to* the ego to diminish unhappiness is a very different enterprise from going *beyond* it. How can we expect to detach ourselves from our egos when success is defined in terms of how our egos should be? In short, it looks as though psychological and spiritual growth aim at entirely incompatable states of affairs: the ego, and that which cannot be identified with it. Furthermore, it looks as though attempts to combine the two kinds of growth can only be counterproductive. There might be talk of enlightenment in *est*, for example, but use of techniques drawn from western psychology ensure that only the ego is affected. As Skynner puts it, approaches of this variety 'mix levels' and so –

> stand in danger of offering a half-truth sufficiently like the real thing to satisfy this deeper (spiritual) hunger without leading to anything more real and even of simply increasing the attachment to the ordinary self.

Compatability

If participants in the new religious movements are to be believed, however, a very different picture emerges. It could of course be the case that an awful lot of people and the movements with which they are associated have got it all wrong. This possibility is discussed later. For the present we introduce historical and testimonial evidence suggesting that psychotherapy can be put to spiritual use; that psychotherapies *are* transformative. We will see what lies behind the observation, reported by Needleman, that:

> The shrinks are beginning to sound like gurus, and gurus are beginning to sound like shrinks.

The general setting is provided by the quite strong tendency for 'secular' psychotherapies to generate or otherwise become associated with spirituality. Contemporaries of Freud – Jung, Groddeck, Reich and Assagioli to name but four – bear witness. So does the increasing extent to which those interested in effecting personal growth have broadened their frontiers. First humanistic psychology (discussed by Vitz in a work with the revealing title *Psychology as Religion*), then the growth or human potential movement, and then, yet more spiritually orientated, transpersonal psychology.

Clare and Thompson go so far to write of 'the inexorable thrust which propels every new therapy into a creed of salvation.' More specifically, they claim:

> Reichian message, Moreno's psychodrama, Rogerian psychotherapy – they each began as a relatively circumscribed approach to helping the mentally distressed and ill and ended up as a programme for living, a philosophical statement and a religious message.

Their overall conclusion is that what was devised as a way of freeing humans from the hold of religion has been put to service in the religious enterprise:

> A search for a way to live, a search which in this century led first to the early, tentative steps of psychoanalysis. . . now, seventy years later, leads back to the religious sensibilities and mysticisms psychoanalysis was intended to supplant.

The tendency for 'secular' psychotherapies to generate spirituality can be yet more vividly illustrated. It seems certain that a not inconsiderable number of new religious movements have in measure been generated by the spiritual potentials of psychotherapy. Dianetics, basically a Freudian psychotherapy, rapidly became subsumed by the Church of Scientology. Much the same kind of development can be seen in the history of Psychosynthesis, Silva Mind Control, Rebirthing, the International Society of Analytical Triology, and even in some manifestations of Primal Therapy and Co-Counselling. Other therapies which have become religious movements include Dianology (Church of Eductivism), Abilitism (Sanatana Dharma Foundation) and Compulsions Analysis (The Process). All these movements might have owed much to the Freudian legacy – but all have transcended it. We can also think of Synanon Foundation Inc., founded in 1958 as an Alcoholics Anonymous alternative, and proclaimed as the Synanon Religion in 1974. Other drug rehabilitation units, especially those employing the Minnesota model, have also developed spiritual features. One well known unit in London appears to be well on the way to becoming the home of a new religious movement.

The most arresting evidence for compatability, however, is provided by movements which have been specifically established as ways of utilising psychological techniques to bring about enlightenment. Self religions, provided for example by Bhagwan and Erhard, draw on western techniques to advance spirituality as envisaged in Eastern terms. More exactly, techniques are used to handle the ego, the entity which stands in the way of monistic realisation of the self itself – the witness of experience, of truth, of the source, of ultimate unitariness.

In this context it is not possible to distinguish between psychological and spiritual growth. The former works to the end of handling the ego in spiritually efficacious fashion. As Bhagwan says,

> This whole life is a challenge to growth. That is the true religion and true psychology, too – because a true religion

> cannot be other than a true psychology. I call that psychology the 'Psychology of the Buddhas'. It gives you a great challenge to be more than you are. It gives you a divine discontent. It makes you aflame with a desire to go higher and higher – not higher than others but higher than yourself.

Indeed, what are called 'spiritual therapies' have worked to bring many to Bhagwan's path. At least until recently, non-sannyasins (Bhagwan's initiates are called 'sannyasins') have come to ashrams to take courses in Rebirthing, Primal, Rajneesh Dynamic Bodywork, Body Awareness, Self Exploration, Hypnotherapy, the 48-Hour Marathon (including bioenergetics, gestalt work and dance), and so on. For many these courses trigger conversion. They lead participants to see what lies beyond the ego.

Werner Erhard's claim is that his seminars facilitate 'de-identification'. In the words of this master:

> The person de-identifies with his mind, de-identifies with his body; he de-identifies with his emotions, he de-identifies with his problems; he de-identifies with his *maya*, he begins to see that he is not the Play.

Techniques employed are highly reminiscent of those found in more secular contexts. Confrontational processes, encounter, gestalt, guided fantasy, catharsis, positive thinking, cognitive therapy, transactional analysis, psychodrama, to name but some, are variously employed. And as with conversion to Bhagwan's path, techniques appear to work. A number of studies show a high incidence of reported benefits. And research on a movement not dissimilar to Erhard's namely Exegesis, shows that many of those who follow the path report experiencing the 'god' that lies within.

Casting his eye over the American scene, Kornfield surmises that 'psychology is a big part of our country's religion right now'. It is difficult to estimate figures, but a conservative guess would be that at least ten million Americans are currently involved with psychospiritual paths, ranging from spiritually significant encounter groups to fully-fledged self religions. Together with the fact that psychotherapies help effect conversion, their spiritual potential, we have seen, is suggested by a number of psychotherapies having generated religious movements. It certainly looks as though psychotherapy can do more than simply strengthen the ego.

Options

We can now look at different ways of explaining how the supposed enemy of spirituality has come to be put to the service of enlightenment. Our question, it will be recalled, is: 'What is it about psychotherapy that has allowed it to be used in this fashion?'

One answer, which will please advocates of the incompatability thesis, is that far from allowing people to go beyond the bounds of personal development psychotherapies are employed to attach participants to a new kind of ego identity – that of dependency on their master. Participants are broken down and made to feel guilty (confrontational techniques); participants are rendered suggestible (cathartic techniques); participants are built up again (positive thinking); and participants are built up in such a way that they can be used to further the ambitions of Bhagwan, Erhard or whoever. Spiritual teachings to do with the self as ultimate or god-like have nothing to do with true spirituality. They are used to motivate participants, to strengthen their egos in accord with the masters' plans, to give religious gloss and santification to what are essentially capitalist ambitions.

A related theme is that spirituality has been added to psychotherapy in order to attract, and then keep, those who are interested in bettering themselves. Some time ago Mowrer wrote –

> Psychiatry is wonderful, religion is wonderful, put them together and you get something better still!

People are attracted to psychotherapies – such as Dianetics, for example. They experience benefits. They go so far, but still feeling dissatisfied they want more. Those who run the therapies therefore engage in the strategy of adding that something more – in the case of Scientology, the possibility of becoming an Operating Thetan, a god-like being. But because Scientology (and most other self religions) continue to present themselves in ways likely to appeal to those interested in psychological growth, they are able to continue to draw their clientele from the psychotherapeutic subculture. Psychotherapeutic presentation, combined with the suggestion that here is something more, functions to ensure numerical success. It is thus not without significance that according to one study, eighty per cent of those attracted to the growth movement have previously been in more secular forms of psychotherapy.

Another theme to do with how psychotherapy can be used in conjunction with spirituality to attract and then keep those interested in perfecting themselves leads us to consider the dynamics of psychotherapeutic processes. It seems clear that many processes are powerful, generating intense and unusual (emotional) experiences. From the work of Schachter and Singer, as well as a number of other experimental studies, we know that experiences of this variety are open to interpretation. What this means is that the relatively inchoate experiences felt during a sannyasin-led group or during an *est* seminar can be moulded or transformed into experiences which accord with the teachings of the movement in question. As a non-sannyasin taking part in a Primal group has told us:

> I felt a gap appear in my mind. It was powerful. Then Bhagwan appeared.

He interpreted his experience in terms of the meanings closest to hand – and so quite naturally felt the presence of Bhagwan. Conversion took place.

It seems incontestable that one of the most important characteristics of psychotherapy which has allowed it to be put to use in the service of enlightenment lies with its capacity to generate unusual experiences. This goes a long way towards explaining why 'secular' psychotherapies can become more spiritual; and why psychotherapeutic techniques are employed in enlightenment seminars; The incompatability critic sees this as generating inauthentic spiritual experiences. Emotions bound up with the ego, in that they 'flood' when the ego is threatened, are the real basis of whatever 'spirituality' is experienced. However, it could equally be the case that psychotherapeutic techniques designed to 'shake' or 'strip' the ego do in fact reveal dimensions of experience which lie beyond the ego and which are of genuine spiritual worth. Whether or not this option is valid cannot be settled from the academic perspective. The possibility that experiences are of the self itself, are of good, cannot be assessed by academic methods of inquiry. However, it perhaps worth nothing that the testimony of major religious traditions, and of a number of interpreters (such as Martin Buber and Victor Turner), apparently support claims of this variety.

Bearing in mind that we cannot arrive at a final decision on the subject, more evidence suggestive of the compatability thesis is that 'secular' psychotherapies often address the ego in ways which accord with what self religions aim to do. Consider scientology, where an aim is to become 'clear' by eradicating 'engrams'. Although traditional Freudian therapies aim to strengthen the ego by eradicating emotional traumas, the fact remains that the processes involved appear to be perfectly compatible with the different aim of going beyond the ego ('engrams', including emotional traumas) to become 'clear'. Dianetics-Scientology shares with Freudian psychotherapy the idea that traumatic incidents are stored until 'relived' ('abreacted'). The psychodynamic process works in both settings to free the ego of harmful influences.

Another illustration of compatability is provided by the importance many psychotherapies and all self religions attach to the act of becoming aware of the operations of the ego. For Erhard 'awareness' is the key to transformation. In the words of an *est* trainer –

> An asshole is a machine that thinks he's not a machine; an *enlightened* man is an asshole that *knows* he is a machine.

It is thus hardly surprising that such seminars draw on psychotherapies (Transactional Analysis, gestalt, confrontational techniques, etc.) which strive to display the extent to which peoples' lives are conditioned by the games they play; by their 'strategies for survival,' unconsciously adopted and now in control. Neither is it surprising to find that Freudian derived psychodynamic theory is here put to use in order to advance self knowledge.

Where scientology might hold that 'engrams' can be erased by catharsis, Erhard, as we have seen, holds that the ego is with us forever – so instead of using catharsis to get rid of distressful experiences processes are employed to make people fully aware of their emotional life. We can best illustrate by reference to the 'platform process' which occurs in most dramatic form in the Exegesis Standard Seminar. After a group catharsis session, which leads participants to feel that they can exercise painful emotions, small groups are lined up on a platform, in front of a large audience, and are told to 'cathart'. They do, sometimes half-vomiting. The seminar trainer then tells them that they have been ridiculous, performing like that in front of so many, taking pride in their ability to break convention in order to get rid of their painful emotions. The trainer goes on to reveal what is really happening:

> If you carry on piling up a load of shit in front of yourself the pile will just get larger and larger.

The point of catharsis, it transpires, is to enable participants to get to know their emotions.

There is much more to be said about compatibilities between psychotherapies and self religions. One obvious point, for example, is that the theory of ego employed by the self religions is virtually identical to that found in behavioural psychology and therapy. Gurdjieff, the father of self religions, taught that 'man is a machine', and he took great delight in meeting J.B. Watson, the father of behavioural psychology. Another important similarity which could be explored is that between cognitive therapy and the role played by 'on the spot' psychoanalysis during psychospiritual seminars. But what of the argument that psychotherapies strengthen the ego?

All we can say on this crucial point is that this does not seem to happen in the self religions. First, the presence of a realm of experience beyond the ego, experienced when the ego is 'cleared' or rendered fully conscious, ensures that ego attachment is not enhanced. The realm ensures that the ego is put in perspective. And second, the presence of such a realm means that the nature of therapies can be transformed. They can be effected by Enlightened masters. This theme is clearly in evidence in Bhagwan's path. Rajneesh spiritual therapy, it is held, goes beyond therapies which allow participants to 'hang on' to their identities, lifestyles and the like. This is because they occur in the 'context' of Bhagwan. It is his spiritual energy which opens up 'the meditative space' in participants. It is his spiritual energy which transforms conventional therapies into techniques which bring people to god. Thus, we are told –

> Rajneesh spiritual therapy is humanistic psychology that has been transformed through being in the hands of an enlightened Master. The way (spiritual therapists) conduct their programmes has its source in the meditative space within themselves that has opened up through being with Him. This inner space is His context.

Most of the self religions reject the term 'psychotherapy'. Representatives claim that their techniques might be derived from mainstream psychotherapy but work in different fashion by virtue of their being utilized by skilled masters or 'context-setters.' Who knows? – other than participants and critics, of course.

PART II

Psychology as Religion

Now let us come at the question from the other side, and look at the spiritual or religious elements that may be present in what is conventionally described as psychotherapy. The most influential psychotherapies, especially those deriving from Freud, are not exactly devoid of religious characteristics. If this is true, the deployment of psychoanalytically based therapies for spiritual ends is an ironic but not an entirely surprising phenomenon. The following interpretation of these therapies will resonate strongly with themes which appeared in the first part of this chapter. Our aim is to show how short a step it is from believing in Freud to believing in the message of self religions. Granted the impact that Freud has made, the religious ingredients of his message go a long way towards explaining why psychotherapeutic techniques are felt to be compatible with, indeed to facilitate, the spiritual search of many in the west.

The first remarkably religious element of psychoanalysis is Freud's theory of the origin of neurosis, in which the psychological downfall of man is given a prehistoric ancestry and eternal significance not unlike the Biblical story of the fall of Adam and Eve. In *Totem and Taboo*, Freud recounts the primal drama which has been imprinted on the human psyche as the prototype of the Oedipal conflict. The son kills the father in order to take possession of a woman he has gathered to himself. Repressed because of its forbiddenness, the conflict is doomed to reappear in the emotional development of every child, and if unresolved will be the cause of adult neurosis. Freud's theory, of the primal deed bears an obvious resemblance to the Genesis story, in which the shaping of human character is a consequence of the original sin of rebellion against the Father. And the role of psychoanalysis in society is also parallel to that played by religion. Whereas salvation in the Judaeo-Christian tradition is dependent on the knowledge of humankind's sinfulness, cure in the psychoanalytic tradition is founded on the unmasking of the origins of human neurosis.

If *Totem and Taboo* did not play a central role in the complex theory of psychoanalysis, the concept of the unconscious, wherein lie the repressed secrets of humankind's forgotten origins, is crucial to the entire Freudian perspective. As well as being the repository of repressed events, wishes and unregenerate instincts, the omniscient unconscious was believed to retain all impressions from earliest experience as well as bearing the imprint of the cosmic death and life urges. The unconscious is therefore a source of mental conflict whose subversive power is weakened by the release of its secrets into consciousness.

The disarming of the unconscious is not a simple matter of 'confession', for the conscious self (ego) actively represses the traumatic and the immoral. 'Infantile amnesia', for example, 'hides the earliest impressions of our mental life from *all of us.*' 'Memories' of disturbing dreams or past events are distorted in an effort to evade the truth. Yet the ego's defensive measures point indirectly to the truth, and Freud believed that 'every former state of memory content may thus be restored.'

It is here that the psychoanalyst takes on the quasi-religious role of the 'seer', for it is he alone, and not even the sincerest of patients, who can understand the true meaning of narratives and dream symbols. In a maxim that precludes the conscious self from guilelessness, Freud stated, 'it is the presence of resistance that is the test of significance, the best clue to the importance of the material under consideration.' Nothing of importance will readily be disclosed by the patient, and the key to the matter is likely to be concealed under layers of self-deception. Only the psychoanalyst possesses the power to discern it. As 'seer', therefore, the psychoanalyst becomes the *uniquely qualified mediator* between humanity's conscious self, which is rooted in the construction of social expectations, and its unconscious reality, which contains a mixture of primordial and primary experience.

That such a process of discernment requires the patient's absolute faith in the powers of the analyst, as much as a willingness to lay bare the contents of his or her unconscious, is unquestionable. The intellectual submission is underscored by the belief that a patient's critical self-reflection hinders the process of cure. In contrast, the analyst, according to Freud, appears as invulnerable as a religious ascetic, whose 'severe discipline', 'courage' and generally 'irreproachable character', is presented to the patient in an impenetrable facade of opacity and 'coldness of feeling'. The gulf between patient and analyst is as important in the process of cure as it is in the purely medical situation, for the principle known as the placebo effect, in which faith in a doctor and his medicine can cure an illness, is undoubtedly paralleled in the psychoanalytic situation. Indeed, Jerome Frank's editorial on 'The Two Faces of Psychotherapy', in which he compares the techniques of psychoanalysis with those of 'religio-magical' healers, makes the same point.

It is finally to Freud's view of religion that we turn to find the most potent comparison of the psychoanalytic experience with the religious one. Freud's attack on religion was basic to his indictment of the church's outworn dogmatic authority and the individual's submission of his rational mind to it. Yet Freud curiously may have reinforced the already prevalent Nineteenth Century romantic view that both disparaged organised religion as false and authoritarian, and recognised religious *feeling* as a pristine state of the soul, observed most authentically in children. In his often quoted response to Romain Rolland, Freud dismissed the 'oceanic feeling' of religious bliss as the consequence of a fixation at the narcissistic stage of infancy, when the child seeks union with the mother. Despite Freud's rejection of this regressive activity, he nonetheless rooted the religious feeling in that great repository of true reality, the unconscious, and identified it with the earliest form of bliss, the selfless union of the child with the parent. Although the moral critique contained in Freud's attack on religion has become history, the fundamentally human source of religious feeling has taken root in the notion of the unconscious.

After Freud, the notion of the unconscious continued to carry religious connotations. In the analytical psychology of Carl Jung, the unconscious as the home of the numinous found direct support. But here, the unconscious is significant less for its experience of religious feeling than for its inheritance of a symbolic universe of religious meaning shared by the human species. Whereas plumbing the unconscious in psychoanalysis aimed at dispelling neuroses and thereby improving social and interpersonal functioning, in Jungian analytical psychology, it is explicitly a method of gaining wisdom and enlightenment.

The specifically European, even Nineteenth Century character of Jungian analytic psychology has had few followers in North America. Several other psychoanalytic offshoots, however – some quite remote from their Freudian roots – have popularised the omniscience of the unconscious, and have sought ways to 'tap' its spiritual, even miraculous, powers.

One variant of psychoanalysis that hovers on the brink of the explicitly religious is Arthur Janov's Primal Therapy, to which we referred in Part I. Positing the existence of a Primal Pain residing in the unconscious, Janov held it to be the cause of layers of debilitating ego defence mechanisms. What is required to get rid of these defences is intensive emotional regression to the universally experienced Primal Pain: the child's fear of the loss of parental love. Reliving the Pain acts to expel it and also to 'shut off' all its attendant neuroses. The patient is often completely cured, it is claimed, in less than three weeks. That a variant of Primal Therapy, called Rebirthing, has established itself in Britain, replete with a supporting system of religious ideas, is predictable. The religious overtones of Janvo's therapy are evident in the beliefs that a primal truth lies hidden in all of us, and that we can vanquish all false ideas and negative behaviour in a ritual catharsis. It could even he argued that rather than cure, what Primal Therapy achieves is conversion.

The similarity of psychological processes and religious conversion is found also in much gentler forms of American psychology. Abraham Maslow's conception of 'peak experiences' in which a broken person is made whole again, brought to a higher threshold of consciousness, and becomes 'god like' in the transcendence of ordinary needs and drives, has much in common with the language of religious conversion. And Erik Erikson's notion of a series of crisis situations, which produce new, ever greater levels of self-understanding, has been shown, in his own biographical accounts of religious figures as well as in appraisals of his developmental psychology, to parallel the gradual process of conversion.

While in many developments of psychoanalysis the religious parallels have remained implicit, in others they have been spelled out clearly. Existential Psychoanalysis, for example, has been directly linked to Zen Buddhism. A leading exponent of this school, Erich Fromm, transmuted the Freudian imperative of 'Where there is Id there shall Ego be,' into a step in the process of enlightenment. Both are methods of dissolving the polarity between the conscious and the unconscious. More important, by positing the unconscious as the authentically universal aspect of being, Fromm believed that its recovery into consciousness 'transforms the mere idea of the universality of man into the living experience of this universality; it is the experiential realisation of humanism.

Concluding Comments

This chapter has surveyed some of the many ways in which religion and psychotherapy seem to interact. The first part showed that, in practice, many of the new religious movements involve techniques that derive from psychotherapy, and that, despite arguments to the contrary, there is a general attitude amongst the adherents of these movements that the therapeutic and spiritual quests are at least compatible, and often mutually supportive. Whilst the second part has shown that even the most orthodox and traditional therapies possess many aspects that can appropriately be termed 'religious.' Whilst we cannot come to a scientific conclusion about the relationship between the two enterprises, it does seem therefore that the boundaries, both conceptual and in terms of practice, are less rigid than has sometimes been argued. It remains likely that psychotherapy does have a legitimate role as at least one subset of possible 'techniques of transformation'.

19

THERAPY AND BEYOND : CONCLUDING THOUGHTS

The contributions to this book have demonstrated some of the ways in which the ideas and methods of the spiritual traditions have been taken up and used by psychologists and psychotherapists. In the theoretical domain, those interested in understanding better the nature of self and of personality have found much, particularly in the traditional literature of Buddhism, to provoke and further their enquiries. When combined with the Buddhist teachings of 'dependent origination' and 'selflessness', constructivist theories of perception' for example, or systems such as Kelly's 'personal construct theory' take on a new urgency and importance, for we are led to investigate the deep beliefs about our own nature that have become dissolved in our day-to-day processes of seeing and thinking. Buddhist teachings provide a mirror that reflects the insights of perceptual psychologists back onto our selves, and that urges us to apply those insights reflexively.

Forming a bridge between theoretical and applied domains, the spiritual traditions have been used to help us formulate better psychologies of emotion than have previously been available. Buddhism traces very simply the way in which illusions concerning self give rise to attachment (to what is congenial to self) and aversion (to what is not,) and shows us how these in turn call forth the whole gamut of discomfitting feelings – guilt, suspicion, greed, cynicism, embarrassment, defensiveness and the rest – that contaminate our relationships at all levels from the personal to the international. We see in stark relief the double-bind that we create for ourselves; first we commit ourselves to an individual philosophy that, by its very nature, generates these emotions; then we forget what the theory is, simply reacting like robots to its programming; and then we top it all off with a theory *about* emotion within which we construe ourselves as passive victims and recipients of bad feelings, without responsibility for either their appearance or their removal. Whilst our right hand is beating us with sticks the left alternately tries to fend off the blows and to massage away the pain. As Welwood says: 'By alienating our own energy, making it 'other' and then judging it negatively, we may come to believe that emotions are demonic, that we have 'monsters' inside us. By treating emotions as an autonomous power, we grant them dominion over us.'

These theoretical insights, inspired by both conceptual and experiential study within the spiritual traditions, have been influential in bringing into being training courses, such as 'the *est* training', 'The Forum', 'Exegesis', 'Insight' and 'Self-transformation' that have proven popular over the last decade, and that are somewhere between philosophical seminars, *sesshins* (prolonged periods of meditation and reflection,) and group psychotherapy. Thus, another way in which the spiritual traditions have had an impact on psychology is in suggesting powerful new technologies for personal enquiry that are appealing to, and suitable for, ordinary, averagely well-adjusted, passably successful people, who wish to dig into 'the meaning of life'. That some of these 'technologies of transformation' make exaggerated claims for themselves ('Instant Enlightenment in Two Weekends!') while others lack suitably wise and compassionate personnel to deliver them, so that the form persists without the original spirit, is unfortunate, and perhaps inevitable. But this should not lead us to make the complementary mistake of dismissing or caricaturing them, nor of underestimating the value that large numbers of people have derived from taking part in them. Through such courses, some of the wisdom, or at least the flavour, of the spiritual traditions has been made available to people who would otherwise have not come across it. And if they serve to whet the appetities of even a proportion of participants – without doing damage to them: a frequent piece of scare-mongering that has no evidence to support it – then they are doing a useful job.

It is when we look at the impact of the spiritual traditions on psychotherapy as such, however, that we find the most matters of contention. For there are legitimate and increasing doubts about the suitability of, say, Buddhist teachings, or *koan* meditation, for people who are confused or unhappy, or who have not, up to a point, mastered the arts of working and relating. It might be useful, therefore, to summarise some of the points at which psychotherapy and the spiritual traditions seem to diverge, and at which distinctions of method and purpose need to be clearly drawn.

Clients most commonly seek therapy because they want to be happier than they are. The prevalence in their lives of some feeling (anxiety, loneliness) is too great, or of another (liveliness, intimacy) too little. Their premise, which the therapist will, by his or her manner, validate, is that they have a problem, and that the appropriate solution is to adjust the balance of feeling, so that they cease to have 'too much' grief or confusion, or 'too little' happiness. To do this, therapist and client explore jointly what it is that is creating the unwanted blockage or glut, and through insight and awareness, by recalling and feeling the pain of past shocks, or by sinking into the unwanted experience in the present, the problem is resolved or the feeling is accepted, and the pain of resistance diminishes. This is a very rough sketch, but not an unfair one, I think.

At the back of both client and therapist's minds, from start to finish, are certain psychological norms or desiderata that guide their progress, provide a benchmark of therapeutic success, and remain unexamined and unchallenged. Well-people, healthy-people are more-or-less rational; are open to their feelings but do not get overwhelmed by them: can cry, but not all the time for a week; care about world hunger, but do not starve themselves; have a 'realistic and positive self-image'; behave well to their parents; care about others but are fairly self-sufficient; get angry when their rights are violated or property stolen; wear shoes to the office; and so on. The implicit contract between helper and helped involves agreement about many such facets of what is normal, healthy and sane – and agreement also that the client needs helping back onto the rails so he or she can live within the guidelines. They spend a limited time together, with a more-or-less specified goal, and an expectation of progress towards it. In most therapeutic schools, openness to experience, self-awareness and self-acceptance are seen as important, or even necessary, means to an end. But the client's aim is to achieve a functional balance between openness and defensiveness. Defences that work, in keeping at bay threatening experiences, can happily be left in place. And the therapist, being the client's servant, should respect his or her wishes and limitations, and not go probing into areas that the client has no felt wish to explore.

On the spiritual path, however, nothing is taken for granted. The premises that underlie the search for happiness, peace, security and self-realisation must themselves be dug up and examined. Nothing can be presupposed, least of all one's assumptions about the nature of Self, or of 'the good life'. The quest is for Truth not Happiness, and if happiness or security or social acceptability must be sacrificed in the pursuit of this ruthless enquiry, then so be it. The spiritual seeker's task is not problem-solving but problem-seeking. Whatever experiences are upsetting must be mounted and ridden in any direction they choose to go, so that the fear that underlies them can be confronted and scrutinised. No thought or feeling or behaviour is 'righter' than any other. It is all grist to the mill – the mill that puts experience to the test, and that relentlessly separates out and discards any belief, however, cherished, that turn out to be unjustified.

In particular, the illusions concerning Self will have to go. While psychotherapy, we might say, seeks to expand the boundary of Me, so that previously alien aspects of myself can be re-espoused, and thereby rendered friendly, the spiritual traditions focus on the boundary itself. Their concern is to help us reality-test the separation of Self from Other, so that it slowly wears thin and patchy and may in a moment of *satori* vanish altogether, like a nightmare on waking. The more I carefully collect the data, and catch it before the sense of separateness has been stirred in to it, the more that sense becomes untenable and unnecessary. In meditations such as *shikan-taza*, or *vipassana*, one cultivates a state of awareness that is intense but choiceless, so that whatever surfaces is experienced fully as it is, neither being clung onto, nor pushed away.

Some of the confusions between what we might call the paths of Happiness (therapy) and Truth (meditation) now become apparent. It happens, for example, that people in therapy experience states of selflessness 'by accident': in moments of self-acceptance, part (at least) of the boundary around Self must dissolve, in order to include the previously banished fear or rage or sadness. Whether such moments are seen for what they are will depend on where the client is looking, and on the perceptiveness and leaning of the therapist they are with. Similarly meditators generate greater self-acceptance 'by accident', as they learn to be able to stand whatever they see about themselves as they sit. And both meditators and therapeutic clients will experience times of serenity as the compulsive patterns of thinking and unease, the products of resistance to oneself, drop away.

In fact, it is often not appreciated by beginners on the path of spiritual growth just how central a role their own mucky, petty emotions are going to play. If they anticipate that meditation will precipitate a steady slide into peacefulness they are in for a shock. Though sitting meditation adopts a pose of stillness, it masks frequent periods of inner turmoil. And the rigour of a Zen monastery, or of a long retreat, are designed precisely to create friction with the ego-emotions, bringing to the surface again and again feelings of frustration, resentment and 'I want/don't want'. Irmgard Schloegl, A Zen teacher in London, is fond of quoting the Buddhist precept:

The Buddha nature is the passions: the passions *are* the Buddha nature. While the Tibetan master Chogyam Trungpa Rinpoche says:

> Unskilled farmers throw away their rubbish and buy from other farmers, but those who are skilled go on collecting their own rubbish, in spite of the bad smell and the unclean work, and when it is ready to be used they spread it on their land, and out of this they grow their crops. And though it is very difficult and unhygienic, as it were, to work on, that is the only way to start. So out of these unclean things comes the birth of the seed which is Realisation.

It can now be seen as well why meditation may not be in the best interests of people who are in therapy. Their 'problem' is that they are struggling not to be overwhelmed by feelings that they are sure dangerous and bad. To stimulate such feelings fully into consciousness, without having strengthened their ability to disidentify with the self-critical voice, is to plunge them into their own particular horror. It requires courage and commitment to 'keep your seat' (as they say in Zen) when the horse is bolting, and if you have not learnt to do so, then the effects will be anything but therapeutic. The meditator must above all learn to make friends with his or her own fearfulness, and develop the ability to sit quietly in its presence without diving for cover. Furthermore, if one is still committed to the *idea* of being in control, then to appear to lose it is terrifying, and one's only recourse is to use to the full whatever defensive ploys of denial or projection or fantasy one has available. In the extreme case, as Laing has reported, even to be understood by someone else can feel like an invasion and a threat.

Even those who are committed to a spiritual path will be swamped from time to time by fear or doubt, as their experience suddenly takes on unfamiliar forms or hues. It is for this reason that a seasoned meditation teacher – someone whom the meditator admires and trusts – is so important, for in times of difficulty the teacher's calm and reassurance will lend the student courage. The same is true of a therapist: his or her ability to look at the client's experience with, in Carl Rogers' phrase, 'fresh and unfrightened eyes' helps the client to see a difficulty through, and not to jump off into renewed defensiveness half-way. And for both therapist and spiritual guide, the only thing that gives them genuine calm – and thereby makes them genuinely trustworthy – is that they have been there themselves. They have walked through the same dark tunnel, found no monsters, and know it to be safe.

But they differ in the breadth and depth of their serenity. The therapist's is like a river, still pools interspersed with white water. The spiritual guides, who know that nothing can threaten them, not even death, because who they truly are is not bounded in either space or time, have a presence like a vast, flat lake. The therapist's self-acceptance is patchy and sporadic, because it is still located within an unquestioned sense of self. He or she can still be shaken by some buried or unprecedented fear. But enlightened people cannot be disturbed by anything, for there is no longer any vestige of a distinction between self and experience. Identified with nothing in particular, they are free to be anything: the feeling of hunger, the pressure of the chair, the broken glass on the forecourt, the disappointed child. They can be touched by everything, for there is nothing to resist. And they can be touched by nothing, for they are a polished mirror on which no reflection can ever leave a mark.

We might conclude from this that while meditation will be inappropriate for many clients, tending to push them further than they are ready, willing or able to go, it offers an invaluable aid to therapists, that ought to be a part of every therapist's initial and on-going training. The products of meditation are insight, awareness, equanimity and magnanimity, and any therapist who declines to undertake a practice that strengthens and expands these vital therapeutic qualities has some explaining to do. Welwood is certainly in no doubt on this point:

> When I studied Rogerian therapy in graduate school, I felt frustrated because I was never taught *how* to develop

'unconditional positive regard' for the client. I was told that this was essential, and it sounded good to me, but it was assumed that I should be able to feel this way toward anyone who walked into my office. What I discovered many years later was that meditation provided a concrete operational method for developing just those ingredients of acceptance and unconditional friendliness that are most essential for successful therapy. A therapist who sits through the subtle, complex twists and turns of his own thoughts and feelings is unlikely to find many of his clients' problems all that aline, shocking or unfamiliar. The more a therapist trusts his own basic goodness underneath his confusion, the more he can help clients find their way between these two aspects of themselves. And the more he can face his own fear, the more fearlessly he can approach his clients' problems as well. . .

The spiritual traditions therefore offer an invitation to psychotherapists to see their training as experiential and continuous, and to appraise their value to their clients in terms of qualities of *being*, rather than the skills and techniques of *doing* or the conceptual understanding of *knowing*. Without such qualities as the tradition Rogerian trinity of genuineness, non-judgemental warmth and compassionate understanding, all the skill and knowledge in the world are unlikely to do any goods. Unfortunately, this is an invitation that many psychotherapists will turn down, for they will find it threatening to both their personal and their professional selves. Personally they will be unwilling to put at risk the workable patchwork of beliefs and evasions that constitute their personalities. While many will also be loath to give up the professional standing that their claim to knowledge and skill gives them, Many therapists are deeply attached to a sense of their own power, control, expertise and understanding, and to accept that these count for little beside the qualities of basic human-heartedness that they cannot affect, and may lack, may be too bitter a pill to swallow. To be asked to inspect and question their own need to be successful, or to have it suggested that such a need is itself neurotic, and a failing in a good therapist, will feel like an attack that must be warded off.

It is probably also true that many therapists are too attached to the drama of neurosis. The spiritual teachers I have met have all shared one delightful quality that is easy to recognise but hard to describe. Seeing both the tragedy of the suffering we are in, and at the same time the irony of a situation in which we ourselves are responsible for the pain we would escape, they are able to communicate both acceptance and humour. On the one hand, they can understand our predicament, show compassion, and do not make us feel small. But on the other, there is a lightness of touch that says 'Come on now. This is all rather silly, isn't?' They see the drama clearly but refuse to buy it, and the twinkle in their eye can somehow help us see for ourselves the home-made, out-of-all-proportion nature of our upset. In short they behave like a loving parent with a child with a burst balloon: they can *comfort* us without *agreeing* with us. They keep sight of the big picture. And sometimes they can help us to laugh at ourselves: to see ourselves as ridiculous, but without putting ourselves down, and to acquire towards ourselves the same attitude of gentle, amused affection that they have towards all emotional absurdity.

Whereas some therapists, like naive parents, get sucked into the turmoil, and, losing their perspective, come to collude with our point of view about how *serious* it all is, and thereby strengthen it. Such therapists may help patients to see into their predicament, but not to see through it. And, understanding the tragedy but not the comedy, they will find the message of the spiritual traditions unappealing, or even frivolous.

For the enlightened master, therapist and client are both in the same boat, whilst for himself and his students there is a very definite distinction. They are looking for something and he's got it (or rather he knows that he's got it, and they don't yet know that they've got it as well.) And it is very clearly his job to help them look for it, and to prevent them looking for it in the wrong places – in an accumulation of intellectual knowledge, for example, or in the deliberate affectation of some lifestyle. In his students' relationship to him there is therefore a degree of respect and honouring that would be out of place in the therapist's consulting room. The master manifests his disillusionment in everything he says and does, though it is not so much the content of his words and actions as the subtle spirit that pervades them that conveys the message. He teaches through his example, his being, as much as through the exercises he sets or the teachings he gives, and as students spend time in his presence, so they hope to pick up something of that quality of being. It simply begins to rub off on them. Thus, while they are earnestly picking away at their own misconceptions, discarding that which is false, so at the same time they are being infected with and inspired by a light, lively, loving intelligence. But 'it's a wise man who knows his own limitations' (as Clint Eastwood said to his superior in one of the Dirty Harry movies), and few therapists would prescribe as part of their therapeutic regime that clients should come and watch them eating their supper, or playing with the cat.

The other big difference between the paths of Happiness and Truth is the extent to which they permeate a seeker's life. Therapy, by and large, concerns itself with the domain of feeling and emotion. Though it may be something in the clients' relationships, their actions, their thinking or their perception that is giving rise to their unhappiness, these aspects of their lives are only investigated or altered so that the reading on the Misery-ometer goes down. If we can reinterpret the hallucinations, or get rid of the phobia, you will Feel Better, and that is the point. But for the spiritual seeker these other domains are made problematic in their own right. In all the Buddhist traditions, though especially in Rinzai Zen's use of the *koan*, the status and value of thought itself is questioned: not just some (weird) thoughts, but all thought. Educated Westerners in particular have been trained to be very good at using the tool called Reason, but have been hopelessly mislead about the limits of its usefulness. We are like surgeons who can wield a scalpel with exquisite skill, but insist on using the scalpel to take a temperature, treat a headache or open a tin of sardines. The *koan* is a device for breaking people of the compulsion to use the scalpel of rational thought on inappropriate problems – the problem in question being 'What am I?' Only after we have blunted a hundred fine-ground blades on the sardine tin, and are blue in the face with frustration and hunger, are we willing to look around, and spot the can-opener that has been on the table the whole time. Beliefs about the nature and function of thought have to be brought to the surface and reappraised.

Likewise our perception of the external world is called into question. Our common-sense attitude to perception is built on the premise that we *receive* it, as a television set receives electromagnetic waves through the air, and turns them into sound and pictures. Embedded in this belief is a clear distinction between inside and outside, Me and Not-Me. But close attention to experience, and particularly to the errors and interpretations it contains, begin to reveal that there is a much closer relationship between Who-I-Am and What-I-See than had seemed to be the case. I am not so much the receiver of my perception as its creator, and therefore I am at some level responsible for it. So in the course of this enquiry the boundary between Self and Other is again eroded and punctured. The sense of self becomes diffused, and 'I' seems to expand to include both other people and, in the limit, everything that I have sensed and known. Where the therapeutic enquiry leads to a reconstruing of the intra-personal, the spiritual enquiry widens to include the interpersonal and ultimately the impersonal worlds. And as it does so, the seeker's orientation shifts from the predominant concern with personal salvation to a broad sense of authorship of every aspect of experience, and a deep concern for all the creatures that 'I' have brought into being.

In summary, we might say that therapy represents a special and limited case of the more general spiritual search, as Newton's Laws of Motion are special cases of Einstein's broader theory of Relativity. The quests for Happiness and for Truth thus share certain features, but aspects of the former are localised, and must not be assumed to apply across the board. Someone starting in therapy may get a taste for self-enquiry that becomes freed from the pursuit of happiness and deepens into a spiritual journey, and this shifting of focus often happens. But a definite change of gear is involved that should not be expected – or even necessarily encouraged – to occur.

There are echoes of the spiritual traditions in all the brands of therapy: it would be surprising if there were not. George Kelly's personal construct approach highlights the way we create our own interpersonal perceptions (and then take them for gospel); Carl Rogers has much to say about openness to one's inner experience and the value of receptivity; Fritz Perls' gestalt therapy stresses the importance of here-and-now attention to detail; Albert Ellis emphasises the fact that unhappiness is caused by errors in our personal philosophies; many movements pick out the importance of non-judgemental attention; Sigmund Freud, of course, started us thinking about the ploys and evasions we use in order to avoid noticing the absurd or threatening aspects of our experience; and so on. But all of them are brought up short at some point by their adherence to a belief or an unexamined assumption that the inexorable Buddhist bulldozer would continue to batter its way through.

As this book has shown, there are many areas of psychology and psychotherapy that are beginning to benefit from contact with the spiritual traditions. But we must be wary in interpreting and applying those traditions, for they are powerful, and not to be treated superficially or lightly. Wilber has pointed out how the parallels between mysticism and modern physics have been exaggerated and trivialised and we would do well to heed his warning in relating psychology and spirituality. Critical caution should prevent us from polluting the rich harvest of insights that is available with our own overenthusiasm, and half-baked preconceptions.